PLAYS FOR PERFORMANCE

*A series designed for
contemporary production and study
Edited by
Nicholas Rudall and Bernard Sahlins*

HENRIK IBSEN

The Wild Duck

In a New Adaptation by
Robert Brustein

Ivan R. Dee
CHICAGO

Library of Congress Cataloging-in-Publication Data:
Ibsen, Henrik, 1828–1906.
    [Vildanden.   English]
    The wild duck / Henrik Ibsen : in a new adaptation by Robert Brustein.
        p.   cm. — (Plays for performance)
    ISBN 1-56663-169-6 (alk. paper). — ISBN 1-56663-170-X (pbk. : alk. paper)
    I. Brustein, Robert Sanford, 1927–   . II. Title. III. Series.
PT8881.I2713   1997
839.8'226—dc21   97-24712

INTRODUCTION

by Robert Brustein

This adaptation of Henrik Ibsen's *The Wild Duck* was prepared for François Rochaix's production of the play by the American Repertory Theatre. My task was to try to chart a course between the stodgy Victorian locutions of the William Archer school and an excessively colloquial modern treatment while also trying to reclaim Ibsen for our time.

My *Wild Duck* is not, therefore, a contemporary reworking of the play—Eugene O'Neill already did that (brilliantly) when he wrote *The Iceman Cometh*. It is rather an attempt to dig a fresh tunnel into the obscure poem buried in its heart. With this play Ibsen was taking a new direction, exploring the intricate relations among characters who work on each other like the various ganglia of a single nervous system. In dramatizing the destructive impact on an average family of a neurotic fanatic who fails to understand the consequences of his "claim of the ideal," Ibsen seems to be satirizing himself and his followers. Not altogether true. He is simply showing, as he often said, that he was more of a dramatic poet and less of a social philosopher than was commonly believed. He was demonstrating through dramatic action that even the most persuasive doctrine must yield to human circumstances.

The Ekdal family, like the wild duck they all cher-

3

ish and nurture, is buried in the "depths of the sea." Any effort to pull them out of the tangled seaweed into the harsh light of reality is bound to result not so much in tragedy as in dissonance—half comic, half tragic, and all the more disturbing because the elements are mixed.

Ibsen called the illusion of his characters "life lies." O'Neill called them "pipe dreams." Both artists believed that while it was essential for humankind to advance beyond the primitive phase in which it now exists, it was also essential to exercise compassion in regard to those unable to face harsh truths. Gregers Werle is looking for a superior being because he lacks any real nobility himself. He needs another to complete him, another to execute his ideas. In mistakenly choosing the illusionist Hjalmar Ekdal as his agent, Gregers proves himself as benighted as any of the people he has come to liberate from their life lies. Does this mean that Ibsen had given up on Ibsenism? He never embraced it— or any other doctrine for that matter. He remains what he always was: an artist beyond politics—elusive, evasive, dangerous, alive.

A word about production. Unlike most of Ibsen's plays of this period, *The Wild Dick* demands two distinct settings—one, the Werle household, the other, the Ekdal studio, complete with an attic housing a menagerie of domestic animals. The Rochaix production staged the first act in a narrow red room, which descended on an elevator to reveal Gina and Hedwig in the Ekdal household (the attic was now a cellar in the orchestra pit). A circular turntable will accomplish the same ends. If you lack either piece of machinery, then you're in for a rather long scene change.

The play is in five acts and therefore longer than most of Ibsen's modern works. It contains some repetition. Don't be afraid to cut. Finally, the obscenity I chose as the last words spoken is not too far from Ibsen's final expletive, though it shocked some audience members and almost all the critics. Given Dr. Relling's sense of disgust over what has transpired and his contempt for Gregers, I'm convinced the phrase is one that, had he not been worried about the censors, Ibsen might have used. But if it bothers you as well, then substitute the less offensive phrase "Oh, go to hell."

CHARACTERS

WERLE, a merchant and manufacturer
GREGERS WERLE, his son
OLD EKDAL
HJALMAR EKDAL, his son, a photographer
GINA EKDAL, Hjalmar's wife
HEDVIG, their daughter, a girl of fourteen
MRS. SOERBY, Werle's housekeeper
RELLING, a doctor
MOLVIK, a former student of theology
PETERSON, Werle's servant
A FAT GUEST
A THIN-HAIRED GUEST
A SHORTSIGHTED GUEST

The Wild Duck

ACT 1

*Werle's house. A rich, comfortably furnished study; book-
cases and upholstered furniture; in the center of the room,
a writing table with papers and documents; lighted lamps
with green shades, giving a subdued light. At the back,
open folding doors with curtains drawn back. Inside is
seen a large and handsome room, brilliantly lighted with
lamps and branching candlesticks. In front, on the right
(in the study), a small private door leads into Werle's office. On the left, in front, a fireplace with a glowing coal
fire, and farther back a double door leading into the dining room.*

*On stage Werle's servant, Peterson, in livery. From the
dining room are heard the hum of conversation and
laughter of many voices. A glass is tapped with a knife; silence follows, and a toast is proposed. Shouts of "Bravo!"
and then again a buzz of conversation.*

A VOICE FROM THE AUDIENCE: Hey, Peterson, what's
going on in there?

PETERSON: *(Lights a lamp on the chimney-place and
places a shade over it. To the audience.)* You mean in
the dining room? The old man's toasting Mrs. Soerby.

AUDIENCE VOICE: So the rumors are true?

PETERSON: The official word is they're just good
friends. He's gotten too creaky for anything more
energetic.

11

AUDIENCE VOICE: Yeah, but they say he was pretty frisky in his day.

PETERSON: That's what they say. This dinner going on inside—it's in honor of his son, Gregers.

AUDIENCE VOICE: The old guy has a son?

PETERSON: He's got a son all right, though you'd never know it. The kid spends all his time up at the Hoidal mill. He didn't come home once in all the time I've worked here. Hold on a second.

(Old Ekdal appears from the right, in the inner room. He is dressed in a threadbare overcoat with a high collar; he wears woolen mittens and carries in his hand a stick and a fur cap. Under his arm, a brown paper parcel. Dirty red-brown wig over his bald dome and small grey mustache.)

PETERSON: *(goes toward him)* Hey, what are you doing here?

EKDAL: *(in the doorway)* I got to get in the office, Peterson.

PETERSON: The office closed an hour ago, and—

EKDAL: Yeah, they told me that at the door. But Graberg's still working in there. Be a good guy and let me in this way, Peterson. *(points toward the door)* I used to come through here all the time.

PETERSON: Well, go ahead . . . *(opens the door)* but be careful when you leave. We got company.

EKDAL: I know, I know! Thanks, Peterson, you're a good friend! Thanks! *(mutters softly)* Asshole! *(he goes into the office; Peterson shuts the door after him)*

AUDIENCE VOICE: Who's the old geezer? One of the clerks?

PETERSON: He does copying jobs here from time to time. You'd never know it now, but he was a real hotshot in his day, old Ekdal.

AUDIENCE VOICE: He looks like he's been dumped on a lot.

PETERSON: He used to be an army officer, you know.

AUDIENCE VOICE: Well I'll be. . . . An army officer!

PETERSON: But then he went into lumber, coal mines, or something like that. They say he once got Mr. Werle in a lot of hot water when they were partners in the Hoidal mill. Old Ekdal and me have guzzled our share of ale together at Madame Ericson's.

AUDIENCE VOICE: He doesn't look like he's got the price.

PETERSON: Oh, it's always my treat. It never hurts to be decent to people in trouble.

AUDIENCE VOICE: He lost all his money?

PETERSON: And worse than that. He went to jail.

AUDIENCE VOICE: He went to jail?!

PETERSON: *(listens)* Button up! They're leaving the table.

(The dining room is thrown open from within. Mrs. Soerby comes out conversing with two gentlemen. Gradually the whole company follows, among them Werle. Last come Hjalmar Ekdal and Gregers Werle.)

MRS. SOERBY: *(in passing, to Peterson)* Tell them to serve the coffee in the music room, Peterson.

13

PETERSON: Yes, madam. *(She goes with the two gentlemen into the inner room, and then out to the right. Peterson goes out the same way.)*

THE FAT GUEST: *(to the Thin-haired Guest)* Whew! What a banquet! Eating all that was hard work!

THE THIN-HAIRED GUEST: In three hours you can gobble a lot.

THE FAT GUEST: Yes, but you pay a price afterward, my friend!

THE SHORTSIGHTED GUEST: I hear they're serving coffee and cordials in the music room.

THE FAT GUEST: Great! Then maybe Mrs. Soerby will play a little number for us.

THE THIN-HAIRED GUEST: *(in a low voice)* As long as it's a number we can dance to!

THE FAT GUEST: Don't worry about that! Bertha doesn't turn her back on old friends. *(they laugh and pass into the inner room)*

(Enter Werle and Gregers.)

WERLE: *(in a low voice)* I don't think anybody noticed, Gregers.

GREGERS: *(looks at him)* Noticed what?

WERLE: You didn't either?

GREGERS: What are you talking about?

WERLE: There were thirteen of us at table.

GREGERS: There were? Thirteen?

WERLE: *(looks toward Hjalmar Ekdal)* Usually we're only twelve. *(going back into the dining room)* This way, gentlemen!

HJALMAR: *(who has overheard the conversation)* It was a mistake to invite me, Gregers.

GREGERS: To my own party? A mistake to ask my best, my only friend?

HJALMAR: I don't think your father approves. I'm a total outsider here.

GREGERS: So it seems. But I had to talk to you, and I'm not down here for long. We've certainly drifted apart since our schooldays. I don't think I've seen you in sixteen or seventeen years.

HJALMAR: That long?

GREGERS: That long. Well, how are you doing? You look well. You've put on a little weight, I see. You're getting a little fat.

HJALMAR: Well, I wouldn't call myself fat. But I've certainly become more substantial than I used to be.

GREGERS: The outer man looks in great condition.

HJALMAR: *(in a tone of gloom)* Ah, but you can't see the inner man! That's a whole different story! Of course you heard about the disaster my family has suffered since I saw you last . . .

GREGERS: *(more softly)* How is your father doing now?

HJALMAR: Let's not talk about it, my friend. He lives with me of course, my poor old father. The miserable fellow doesn't have anybody else in the world. But let's talk about pleasant things. Tell me how you're doing up at the sawmill.

GREGERS: It's wonderfully solitary. Lots of time to think. About a lot of things. Come, let's get comfortable. *(he seats himself in an armchair by the fire and signals Hjalmar into another alongside it)*

HJALMAR: *(sentimentally)* Gregers, I'm really grateful you invited me to your father's house. It means you don't bear a grudge against me any more.

GREGERS: *(surprised)* What makes you think I ever had a grudge against you?

HJALMAR: At first you did.

GREGERS: At first?

HJALMAR: After the great catastrophe. It was perfectly understandable. Your father came very close to being implicated in that—that awful business.

GREGERS: But why would I bear you a grudge? Who put that idea in your head?

HJALMAR: Your father told me.

GREGERS: *(starts)* My father! He did? Is that why I never heard a single word from you in all that time?

HJALMAR: Yes.

GREGERS: Not even to tell me about your decision to be a photographer?

HJALMAR: Your father said it would be better if I didn't write to you at all, about anything.

GREGERS: *(looking straight before him)* Well, well, maybe he was right. But tell me, Hjalmar, are you happy now? Doing what you're doing?

HJALMAR: *(with a little sigh)* Well, yes, yes, I don't complain. It was a little peculiar at first, you know, such a new kind of life. But then the old life had

16

become impossible. My father's total ruin, the shame, the disgrace.

GREGERS: *(affected)* Yes, yes, I know.

HJALMAR: I couldn't stay in school. We didn't have any money at all. Actually, there were a lot of debts—mostly to your father, I believe.

GREGERS: Hm—

HJALMAR: So it was best to break with my old way of life, my friendships. It was your father who talked me into it. And since he took such an interest in me . . .

GREGERS: My father took an interest in you?

HJALMAR: Didn't you know that? Where do you think I got the money to study photography, to furnish a studio and set myself up? All that costs a bundle, you know.

GREGERS: And my father paid for everything?

HJALMAR: Yes, old friend, didn't you know? I thought he said he wrote you about it.

GREGERS: He didn't say a word about doing anything for you. He must have forgotten. We only exchange letters about business. So it was my father who—!

HJALMAR: Of course. He didn't want it known. But he was the one. And he was the one who made it possible for me to get married, too. *(pause)* You didn't know that either?

GREGERS: Not a thing. *(shakes him by the arm)* But, my dear Hjalmar, I can't tell you how happy this makes me. Happy and a little guilty. I think I may have done my father an injustice. This proves he may have a heart after all. It shows he has a little conscience—

HJALMAR: Conscience?

GREGERS: Yes, yes—whatever you want to call it. Anyway, I'm really glad to hear this. So you're a married man now, Hjalmar! That's more than I can say about myself. I assume you're happy in your marriage?

HJALMAR: Totally happy. I have the best, the most capable wife a man could ask for. And she's not completely uneducated either.

GREGERS: *(rather surprised)* I would guess not.

HJALMAR: You see, life itself is a learning experience. She has her daily talks with me—and we know a lot of intelligent people. You would hardly recognize Gina anymore.

GREGERS: Gina?!

HJALMAR: Yes. You don't remember her name was Gina?

GREGERS: Which Gina? I don't know what—

HJALMAR: You forgot she used to work here?

GREGERS: *(surprised)* You mean Gina Hansen—?

HJALMAR: Yes, of course. Gina Hansen.

GREGERS: —our housekeeper during the last year my mother was sick?

HJALMAR: That Gina. But my dear friend, I'm sure your father told you I was married.

GREGERS: *(who has risen)* Oh yes, I remember he said something. But not that it was— *(walking about the room)* Wait a minute—maybe he did—now that I

18

think of it. My father's letters are always so short. . . . *(half seats himself on the arm of the chair)* But tell me, Hjalmar—it's really odd—how did you get to meet Gina—I mean, your wife?

HJALMAR: Very simple. You remember Gina didn't stay here long—everything was so chaotic at that time, what with your mother being sick and all. Gina didn't feel up to it, so she gave her notice and left. It was the year before your mother died—or maybe it was the same year.

GREGERS: It was the same year. I was up at the mill then. But after that—?

HJALMAR: After that, Gina went to live with her mother, Mrs. Hansen, a fine, hard-working woman who runs a little restaurant. She had a room for rent too, a very comfortable room.

GREGERS: And you were lucky enough to rent it, I suppose?

HJALMAR: Yes. In fact, it was your father who told me it was available. And that's how I got to know Gina.

GREGERS: And it was then you fell in love?

HJALMAR: Yes. It doesn't take long for young people to fall in love.

GREGERS: *(rises and moves about a little)* Tell me, was it after you got engaged—was it then that my father—I mean was it then that you started your photography?

HJALMAR: Exactly. I wanted to get going in a profession and set up house as soon as possible. And your father and I agreed that this photography business was the best way. Gina thought so too.

Oh, and there was another thing in its favor. By luck, Gina knew how to retouch photographs.

GREGERS: That *was* lucky.

HJALMAR: *(pleased, rises)* Yes, wasn't it? A great stroke of luck?

GREGERS: Yes, a great stroke of luck. My father seems to have proven himself a real provider for you.

HJALMAR: *(with emotion)* He did not desert the son of his old friend in his hour of need. He has a good heart, you know.

MRS. SOERBY: *(enters, arm in arm with Werle)* Don't be stubborn, Mr. Werle. You mustn't keep staring into those lights. It's not good for your eyes.

WERLE: *(lets go her arm and passes his hand over his eyes)* You're right, you know.

MRS. SOERBY: *(to the guests in the other room)* Come in this room, please, if you want a glass of punch, gentlemen.

THE FAT GUEST: *(comes up to Mrs. Soerby)* You haven't abolished our sacred right to smoke, have you?

MRS. SOERBY: Sorry. There's no smoking in here. It's Mr. Werle's sanctum.

THE THIN-HAIRED GUEST: When did you enact these laws against cigars, Mrs. Soerby?

MRS. SOERBY: After our last dinner, Chamberlain, when certain people went a little too far.

THE THIN-HAIRED GUEST: And we're not allowed to go a little too far any more, Madame Berta? Not the least bit?

MRS. SOERBY: Not the least bit, Mr. Balle.

(Most of the guests have assembled in the study; servants hand round glasses of punch.)

WERLE: *(to Hjalmar, who is standing beside a table)* What are you examining so intently, Ekdal?

HJALMAR: Only an album, Mr. Werle.

THE THIN-HAIRED GUEST: *(who is wandering about)* Ah, photographs! That's right up your alley, isn't it?

THE FAT GUEST: *(in an armchair)* Have you brought any of your own pictures with you?

HJALMAR: No, I haven't.

THE FAT GUEST: You should have. Looking at pictures helps the digestion.

THE THIN-HAIRED GUEST: And it contributes to the entertainment too, you know.

THE SHORTSIGHTED GUEST: And all contributions are gratefully received.

MRS. SOERBY: The Chamberlains think that everyone has to pay for his dinner, Mr. Ekdal.

THE FAT GUEST: It's only fair when the dinner's so good.

THE SHORTSIGHTED GUEST: Survival of the fittest, my friend, survival of the fittest.

MRS. SOERBY: You're right!

(They continue the conversation with laughter and joking.)

GREGERS: *(softly)* Join in the fun, Hjalmar.

HJALMAR: *(writhing)* What do I have to talk about?

THE FAT GUEST: Don't you think, Mr. Werle, that Tokay is one of the healthiest wines?

WERLE: *(by the fire)* I can certainly vouch for the Tokay you drank this evening. It's an excellent year, one of the best. Of course you noticed that.

THE FAT GENTLEMAN: Yes, it had a remarkably delicate flavor.

HJALMAR: *(shyly)* Is there a difference between the years?

THE FAT GUEST: *(laughs)* That's a good one!

WERLE: *(smiles)* Good wine is wasted on you.

THE THIN-HAIRED GUEST: Tokay is like photography, Mr. Ekdal. Both need sun, right?

HJALMAR: Yes, light is certainly important.

MRS. SOERBY: And it's the same with Chamberlains. They also like to bask in the sun—especially at court.

THE THIN-HAIRED GUEST: That joke has whiskers on it!

THE SHORTSIGHTED GUEST: Mrs. Soerby is coming out of her shell tonight—

THE FAT GUEST: Yes, at our expense. *(holds up his finger reprovingly)* Shame on you, Madame Berta!

ALL THE CHAMBERLAINS: Shame on you!

MRS. SOERBY: And I agree there's a big difference between the years. The older vintages are the best.

THE SHORTSIGHTED GUEST: Do you consider me one of the older vintages?

MRS. SOERBY: Far from it.

THE THIN-HAIRED GUEST: What about me, sweet Mrs. Soerby—?

THE FAT GUEST: And what about me? What vintage do we belong to?

MRS. SOERBY: The very sweetest, gentlemen. *(She sips a glass of punch. The gentlemen laugh and flirt with her.)*

(Peterson carries refreshment trays into the dining room.)

WERLE: Mrs. Soerby can always wriggle out of a difficult situation. Keep your glasses, gentlemen. Peterson, pour some more wine. Gregers, why don't we have a glass together? *(Gregers does not move)* Won't you join us, Ekdal? I didn't get a chance to drink with you at dinner.

(Old Ekdal comes out of the office.)

WERLE: *(involuntarily)* Ugh!

(The laughter and talk among the guests cease. Hjalmar starts at the sight of his father, puts down his glass, and turns toward the fireplace.)

EKDAL: *(does not look up but makes little bows to both sides as he passes, murmuring)* Beg your pardon, come the wrong way. Door's locked—door's locked. Beg your pardon. *(he goes out by the back, to the right)*

GREGERS: *(open-mouthed and staring, to Hjalmar)* Surely that wasn't—!

THE FAT GUEST: What is it? Who was that?

THE SHORTSIGHTED GUEST: *(to Hjalmar)* Did you know that man?

HJALMAR: I don't know—I didn't see him—

THE FAT GUEST: What's come over everybody? *(he joins another group who are talking softly)*

MRS. SOERBY: *(enters and whispers to Peterson)* Give him something to take home with him—something nourishing, you hear?

PETERSON: *(nods)* I'll take care of it. *(goes out)*

GREGERS: *(softly and with emotion, to Hjalmar)* So that was him!

HJALMAR: Yes.

GREGERS: And you stood there and denied you even knew him!

HJALMAR: *(whispers vehemently)* What else could I—!

GREGERS: You didn't acknowledge your own father?

HJALMAR: *(with pain)* Oh, if you were in my place—

THE THIN-HAIRED GUEST: *(approaching Hjalmar and Gregers in a friendly manner)* Aha! Reliving old college memories, are you? Would you like a cigar, Mr. Ekdal? Can I give you a light? Oh, I forgot, we can't—

HJALMAR: No, thank you. I don't—

THE FAT GUEST: Is there a nice little poem you could recite to us, Mr. Ekdal? You used to have a talent for that.

HJALMAR: I'm sorry. I can't remember one.

THE FAT GUEST: Well, that's too bad. Well, what shall we do, Balle?

(Both gentlemen move away and pass into the other room. The conversation inside among the guests, which has been carried on in a low tone, now swells into unconstrained joviality.)

HJALMAR: *(gloomily)* Gregers, I have to go! When a man has been crushed by the hand of fate, he can't— Say goodnight to your father for me.

24

GREGERS: Yes, yes. You're going straight home?

HJALMAR: Yes. Why do you ask?

GREGERS: Because I might come over later.

HJALMAR: No, don't do that. Don't come to my place. You'll find my surroundings a little depressing, Gregers, especially after such a sumptuous banquet. We can always meet somewhere in town.

MRS. SOERBY: *(who has quietly approached)* Are you leaving, Ekdal?

HJALMAR: Yes.

MRS. SOERBY: Remember me to Gina.

HJALMAR: Thanks. I will.

MRS. SOERBY: And tell her I'm coming to see her one of these days.

HJALMAR: Yes, thank you. *(to Gregers)* Stay here. I'll just slip out unobserved. *(he saunters away, then into the other room, and so out to the right)*

MRS. SOERBY: *(softly to Peterson)* Did you give the old man something nice?

PETERSON: Yes, I sent him off with a bottle of cognac.

MRS. SOERBY: You might have chosen something else.

PETERSON: No, Mrs. Soerby, cognac is what he likes best in the world.

(Mrs. Soerby goes back into the dining area, out to the right. Gregers remains standing by the fire. Werle is looking for something on the writing table, hoping that Gregers will go; but Gregers does not move. Werle goes toward the door.)

GREGERS: Father, can I talk to you for a minute?

WERLE: *(stops)* What's up?

GREGERS: There's something I have to say.

WERLE: Can't it wait until we're alone together?

GREGERS: No, it can't. It's possible we'll never be alone again.

WERLE: *(drawing nearer)* What does that mean?

(During what follows, a piano is faintly heard from the distant music room.)

GREGERS: Why has that family been allowed to fall apart so miserably?

WERLE: You mean the Ekdals, I suppose.

GREGERS: Yes, I mean the Ekdals. Lieutenant Ekdal and you were once so close.

WERLE: Much too close. I've been paying for that for years. It's his fault that my reputation has been stained.

GREGERS: *(softly)* Are you sure he was the only one to blame?

WERLE: Who else, for heaven's sake—?

GREGERS: You were partners in that big timber deal—

WERLE: But wasn't it Ekdal who drew up the map of the land we bought—that careless inaccurate map? Wasn't it Ekdal who illegally cut down timber on government property? The whole management was his responsibility. I knew absolutely nothing about what Lieutenant Ekdal was doing.

GREGERS: Lieutenant Ekdal seems to have known absolutely nothing about what he was doing.

WERLE: That's possible. But they found him guilty and acquitted me.

GREGERS: Yes, it's true they never proved anything against you.

WERLE: An acquittal is an acquittal. Why are you raking up these old miseries that have turned my hair prematurely grey? Is that what you've been brooding about up there, all these years? Here in town, I can assure you, Gregers, the whole thing has been long forgotten—at least as far as I'm concerned.

GREGERS: But those miserable Ekdals—

WERLE: What was I supposed to do for them? When Ekdal got out of prison he was a total wreck, beyond all help. There are people in this world who dive to the bottom as soon as they get a couple of slugs in their body, and never resurface. You can take my word for it, Gregers, I've done everything possible without exposing myself to suspicion and gossip—

GREGERS: Suspicion? I see.

WERLE: I give Ekdal copying work for the office, and I pay him far, far more than he's worth—

GREGERS: (without looking at him) That I don't doubt.

WERLE: You're smirking? You think I'm lying? Well, I can't prove it by my books. I never enter payments like that.

GREGERS: (smiles coldly) No, there are certain things it's best not to record.

WERLE: *(taken aback)* What is that supposed to mean?

GREGERS: *(more confidently)* Have you written down what it cost you to teach Hjalmar Ekdal photography?

WERLE: Why should I keep records of that?

GREGERS: I know it was you who paid for his training. And I also know it was you who helped him set up his house.

WERLE: So how can you say I've done nothing for the Ekdals? Those people have cost me plenty.

GREGERS: Have you entered any of these expenses in your books?

WERLE: Why do you keep asking that?

GREGERS: I have my reasons. Now tell me: the time you got so interested in your old friend's son— wasn't that right before his marriage?

WERLE: For Christ's sake, after all these years, how am I supposed to—?

GREGERS: You wrote me a letter around that time—a business letter, naturally—and in a postscript you mentioned—ever so briefly—that Hjalmar Ekdal had married a Miss Hansen.

WERLE: Yes, that's right. That was her name.

GREGERS: What you didn't mention was that this Miss Hansen was Gina Hansen, our former housekeeper.

WERLE: *(with a forced laugh of derision)* No. To tell the truth, it never occurred to me that you were particularly interested in our former housekeeper.

GREGERS: I wasn't. But *(lowers his voice)* there were others in this house who were particularly interested in her.

WERLE: What do you mean by that? *(flaring up)* You don't mean me, I hope?

GREGERS: *(softly but firmly)* Yes, I mean you.

WERLE: And you dare to ...! You presume to ...! That ungrateful hound—that photographer— where does he get off making such accusations!

GREGERS: Hjalmar never breathed a word to me about this. I don't think he had even the faintest suspicion.

WERLE: Then where did you get it from? Who put such idiotic notions in your head?

GREGERS: My poor mother told me—the last day I saw her alive.

WERLE: Your mother! I should have guessed! You and she—you always stuck together. It was she who turned you against me, from the very beginning.

GREGERS: No, it was her suffering and humiliation that broke her down and finally killed her.

WERLE: Oh, she didn't suffer all that much. No more than most people. But it's no use dealing with morbid, neurotic creatures—I've learned that to my cost. ... And so you've been nursing these stupid suspicions—raking up all kinds of ancient rumors and slanders against your own father! I really think you might find something more useful to do at your age, Gregers.

GREGERS: I would think so too.

29

WERLE: It might make your mind a little easier. Easier than it seems now. What's the sense of living up at the mill, year in and year out, slaving away like a common clerk, and never wanting a penny more than your monthly salary? It's simply ridiculous.

GREGERS: I wish I could be so certain of that.

WERLE: I know what's up with you. You want to be independent; you don't want to rely on me for anything. As it happens, you now have an opportunity to gain your independence, to be your own master in every way.

GREGERS: Really? How?

WERLE: When I wrote to you I had particular reasons for asking you to come home. . . .

GREGERS: What were the reasons? I've been waiting all day to find out.

WERLE: I want you to enter the firm, as a partner.

GREGERS: Me? A partner?

WERLE: Yes. We wouldn't have to see each other that much. You could run the business here in town, and I could move up to the factory.

GREGERS: You'd do that?

WERLE: Yes. Actually, I'm not able to work as much as before. I have to be careful of my eyes, Gregers. They've been giving me some trouble.

GREGERS: Your eyes have always been weak.

WERLE: Nothing like now. Besides, there are certain circumstances that make it desirable for me to move up there—at least for a while.

GREGERS: This is a brand new idea.

WERLE: Listen, Gregers, there are many things standing between us. But after all, we are father and son. Surely we can come to some sort of understanding.

GREGERS: You mean, in the eyes of the world?

WERLE: Well, even that would be an improvement. What do you say, Gregers? Do you think it's possible? Huh?

GREGERS: *(looking at him coldly)* There is something behind this.

WERLE: What do you mean?

GREGERS: You want to use me in some way.

WERLE: When two people are as close as we are, they can always be useful to each other.

GREGERS: That's what people say.

WERLE: I want you to stay home with me for a while. I'm a lonely man, Gregers. I've been lonely all my life. But it's worse now that I'm getting old. I need someone close to me. . . .

GREGERS: You have Mrs. Soerby.

WERLE: Yes, I have her. And she's become almost indispensable, to tell you the truth. She is lively and good-natured. She cheers up the house, and that means a lot to me.

GREGERS: Well then, you've got everything going for you.

WERLE: Yes, but I don't think it will last. A woman in her situation could easily find herself compromised in the eyes of the world. It doesn't do my reputation any good, either.

GREGERS: Oh, anyone who gives such great dinner parties doesn't have to worry about public opinion.

WERLE: Yes, but what about her, Gregers? I'm really worried she won't put up with it much longer. Even if she did—even if she were willing to brave the gossip and the scandal out of love for me . . . You have a strong sense of justice, Gregers, what do you think?

GREGERS: *(interrupts him)* Let's get to the point: are you thinking of marrying her?

WERLE: What if I were? What then?

GREGERS: Right, what then?

WERLE: Would you be completely opposed to it?!

GREGERS: Of course not. Not at all.

WERLE: I didn't know if your devotion to your mother's memory—

GREGERS: I'm not a neurotic.

WERLE: Well, whether you are or not, you've lifted a great load off my mind. I'm so happy I can count on your support in this matter.

GREGERS: *(looking intently at him)* Now I see how you want to use me.

WERLE: Use you? What an expression!

GREGERS: Oh, let's not mince words—not when we're alone, anyway. *(with a short laugh)* Well, well. So that's why you wanted me in town. For Mrs. Soerby's sake. We had to pretend to be a family—

to pose for a picture of domestic bliss! That would be something new.

WERLE: How dare you take that tone with me!

GREGERS: Were we ever a family here? Not that I can remember. But now you need to create a big display. What a stage climax it will be when people hear that the son has hurried home, on the wings of filial piety, to attend his grey-haired old father's wedding dinner. What happens then to all those rumors about the wrongs the poor dead mother suffered? They go up in smoke. Her son evaporates them with one simple gesture.

WERLE: Gregers, I don't think there's anyone in the world you hate as much as me.

GREGERS: *(softly)* I've seen you up close.

WERLE: You've seen me with your mother's eyes. *(lowers his voice a little)* But you forget her eyes were— clouded now and then.

GREGERS: *(quivering)* I know what you're getting at. But who was to blame for that unfortunate weakness? You, and all those women! The last being that girl you passed off on Hjalmar Ekdal, when you were good and finished with her—ugh!

WERLE: *(shrugs his shoulders)* Word for word like your mother!

GREGERS: *(without heeding)* And there he is, a big, trusting, unsuspecting baby, surrounded by all this treachery—living under the same roof with such a creature, and not having the slightest idea that what he calls his home is built upon a lie! *(comes a step nearer)* When I look at your past history, I see a battlefield strewn with shattered lives.

33

WERLE: I'm beginning to think that the gulf between us is much too wide.

GREGERS: *(bowing, with self-command)* I've noticed the same thing, so I will take my hat and go.

WERLE: You're leaving?! Leaving the house?

GREGERS: Yes. For I see my purpose in life at last.

WERLE: And what is that?

GREGERS: You'd only laugh if I told you.

WERLE: A lonely man doesn't laugh so easily, Gregers.

GREGERS: *(pointing toward the background)* Look, father, the Chamberlains are playing blindman's buff with Mrs. Soerby. Goodnight and goodbye. *(He goes out by the back to the right. Sounds of laughter and merriment from the company, who are now visible in the outer room.)*

WERLE: *(muttering contemptuously after Gregers)* Ha! Poor devil. And he says he's not a neurotic!

ACT 2

Hjalmar Ekdal's studio, a good-sized room. On the right, a sloping roof composed of large panes of glass, half-covered by a blue curtain. In the right-hand corner, at the back, the entrance door; farther forward, on the same side, a door leading to the sitting room. Two doors on the opposite side, and between them an iron stove. At the back, a wide double sliding door. The studio is plainly but comfortably set up and furnished. Between the doors on the right, standing out a little from the wall, a couch with a table and some chairs; on the table, a lighted lamp with a shade; beside the stove, an old armchair. Photographic instruments and apparatus of different kinds lie about the room. Against the back wall, to the left of the double door, stands a bookcase containing a few books, boxes, and bottles of chemicals, instruments, tools, and other objects. Photographs and small articles, such as paint brushes, paper, and so forth, lie on the table.

Gina Ekdal sits on a chair by the table, sewing. Hedvig is sitting on the sofa, with her thumbs in her ears, reading a book, her hands shading her eyes.

GINA: *(glances once or twice at Hedvig, as if with secret anxiety, then says)* Hedvig! *(Hedvig does not hear; Gina repeats more loudly)* Hedvig!

HEDVIG: *(takes away her hands and looks up)* Mother?

GINA: Hedvig dear, you have to stop reading now.

HEDVIG: Oh mother, just a little more? Just a few more pages?

35

GINA: No, no, it's time to put the book away. Your father doesn't like it. He never reads at night.

HEDVIG: *(shuts the book)* No, daddy doesn't read much at all.

GINA: *(puts aside her sewing and takes up a pencil and a little account book from the table)* Do you remember how much we paid for butter today?

HEDVIG: One crown sixty-five.

GINA: That's right. One crown sixty-five. *(writes it down)* It's awful the amount of butter we go through in this house. Then there was the smoked sausage, and the cheese—let's see— *(writes)* —and the ham— *(adds it up)* That comes to—

HEDVIG: Don't forget the beer.

GINA: Yes, the beer. *(writes)* It all adds up! But we can't manage with less.

HEDVIG: But you and I didn't need a hot dinner. Daddy was out.

GINA: Yes, that was a savings. And then I took in eight crowns fifty for the photographs.

HEDVIG: Really! That much?

GINA: Eight crowns fifty exactly.

(Silence. Gina takes up her sewing again. Hedvig takes paper and pencil and begins to draw, shading her eyes with her left hand.)

HEDVIG: Isn't it exciting to think of daddy at Mr. Werle's big dinner party?

GINA: Yes, but he's not really a guest of Mr. Werle. The son invited him. *(after a pause)* We don't have anything to do with that Mr. Werle.

36

HEDVIG: I can't wait for daddy to come home. He promised to ask Mrs. Soerby for something nice for me.

GINA: Yes, there's plenty of good stuff in that house, I can tell you.

HEDVIG: *(goes on drawing)* And I am a little hungry, I think.

(Old Ekdal, with the paper parcel under his arms and another parcel in his coat pocket, comes in by the entrance door.)

GINA: Why are you so late, grandfather?

EKDAL: They had the office door locked. And I had to go through—hm.

HEDVIG: Did you get some more copy work, grandfather?

EKDAL: All this. Just look.

GINA: That's wonderful.

HEDVIG: And you have another package in your pocket too.

EKDAL: What? Oh that's nothing, nothing. *(puts his stick away in a corner)* This will keep me busy for a long time, Gina. *(he opens one of the sliding doors in the back wall a little)* Quiet! *(he peeps into the room for a moment, then pushes the door carefully shut again)* Hee-hee! They're all asleep down there. And she's gone into the basket all by herself. Hee-hee!

HEDVIG: Isn't she cold in that basket, grandfather?

EKDAL: Of course not! Cold? With all that straw? *(goes toward the farther door on the left)* Are there any matches here?

GINA: On the shelf.

(Ekdal goes into his room.)

HEDVIG: Isn't it nice that grandfather got all that copy work?

GINA: Yes, poor old grandfather, he'll have a bit of pocket money.

HEDVIG: And he won't have to sit all afternoon in that awful restaurant of Mrs. Eriksen.

GINA: Not any more he won't. *(short silence)*

HEDVIG: Do you think they're still eating dinner?

GINA: Goodness knows. Probably.

HEDVIG: Think of all the delicious things daddy's eating! He's sure to be in a good mood when he comes home. Don't you think so, mother?

GINA: Yes, but wouldn't it be nice if we could tell him we've rented the room—

HEDVIG: We don't have to do that tonight.

GINA: Oh, it would be such a help. It's no use empty.

HEDVIG: I mean we don't have to tell him tonight. Daddy will be in a good mood anyway. Better to keep news of the room for another time.

GINA: *(looks across at her)* You like having nice things to tell your father when he comes home at night?

HEDVIG: Yes, because that somehow makes everything more pleasant.

GINA: *(thinking to herself)* Yes, that's true enough.

(Old Ekdal comes in again and is going out by the nearest door to the left.)

38

GINA: *(half turning in her chair)* Do you want something in the kitchen, grandfather?

EKDAL: Yes, yes, I do. Don't make any fuss. *(goes out)*

GINA: I hope he's not poking the fire in there. *(waits a moment)* Hedvig, go and see what he's up to.

(Ekdal comes in again with a small jug of steaming hot water.)

HEDVIG: Have you been heating some water, grandfather?

EKDAL: Hot water, yes. Need it for something. Have to write, and the ink's as thick as porridge—hm.

GINA: But have some supper, first. It's all ready in there.

EKDAL: Can't be bothered with supper, Gina. Too busy. Don't let anyone in my room. No one at all—hm. *(he goes into his room; Gina and Hedvig look at each other)*

GINA: *(softly)* Where do you think he got the money from?

HEDVIG: Maybe from Graberg.

GINA: I don't think so. Graberg always sends the money to me.

HEDVIG: Then he must have gotten a bottle on credit somewhere.

GINA: Who would give your poor grandfather credit?

(Hjalmar Ekdal, in an overcoat and grey felt hat, comes in from the right.)

GINA: *(throws down her sewing and rises)* Back already, Ekdal?

HEDVIG: *(at the same time jumping up)* You've come home so soon, daddy!

HJALMAR: *(taking off his hat)* Yes, most of the guests were leaving.

HEDVIG: This early?

HJALMAR: Yes, it was a dinner party, you know. *(he takes off his overcoat)*

GINA: Let me help.

HEDVIG: Me too. *(they take off his coat; Gina hangs it up on the back wall)*

HEDVIG: Were there a lot of people there, daddy?

HJALMAR: Not so many. The table held about twelve or fourteen.

GINA: And you talked with all of them?

HJALMAR: Oh yes, a little. But Gregers took up most of my time.

GINA: Is Gregers as ugly as ever?

HJALMAR: Well, he's not much to look at. Is the old man home yet?

HEDVIG: Yes, he's busy writing in his room.

HJALMAR: Did he say anything?

GINA: No, what about?

HJALMAR: He didn't say anything about—? I heard he'd been with Graberg. I'll drop in on him for a moment.

GINA: No, no, better not.

HJALMAR: Why not? Did he say he didn't want me in there?

GINA: He doesn't want to see anybody tonight—

HEDVIG: *(making signs)* Hm-hm!

GINA: *(not noticing)* —he came in for some hot water—

HEDVIG: Hm—hm!

HJALMAR: Aha! Then he's probably—

GINA: Yes, he's probably—

HJALMAR: Good God! My poor grey-haired old father! Well, well, he needs whatever pleasures he can get.

(Old Ekdal, in an indoor coat and with a lighted pipe, comes from his room.)

EKDAL: You're home? Thought I heard you talking.

HJALMAR: Yes, I just came in.

EKDAL: You didn't see me, did you?

HJALMAR: No, but I heard you'd passed through—so I thought I'd follow.

EKDAL: Hm—nice of you, Hjalmar. Who were they, all those people?

HJALMAR: Oh, all types. There was Chamberlain Flor, and Chamberlain Balle, and Chamberlain Kaspersen, and Chamberlain—whatever his name is—I don't know who else—

EKDAL: *(nodding)* Hear that, Gina! All of them chamberlains!

GINA: Yes, I hear that house has gotten very fancy.

HEDVIG: Did anyone sing, daddy? Or recite anything?

HJALMAR: No, they only talked nonsense. They wanted me to recite something, but I wasn't going to do that.

EKDAL: Couldn't persuade you, eh?

GINA: Oh, you might have recited something.

HJALMAR: No, I don't always have to be available to perform. *(walks about the room)* That's not for me, anyway.

EKDAL: No, no, Hjalmar's not for the asking, he isn't.

HJALMAR: I don't see why I should be required to entertain people the few times I go out. Let other people exert themselves a little. These people go from one big house to another, gorging and guzzling one night after the other. Let them do something in return for all the good meals they gobble down.

GINA: You didn't say that?

HJALMAR: *(humming)* Hm, hm, hm—well, I did give them a good piece of my mind.

EKDAL: Not the chamberlains?

HJALMAR: Why not? I was pretty subtle about it. After that, we had a little discussion about Tokay.

EKDAL: Tokay! There's a wine for you!

HJALMAR: It can be a good wine. But of course you know the vintages are all of different quality. Everything depends on how much sunshine the grapes get.

GINA: There isn't anything you don't know, Hjalmar.

EKDAL: And did they argue with you about that?

HJALMAR: They tried to. But they were told it was just the same with chamberlains—everything depends on the year.

GINA: How do you think up such things!

EKDAL: Hee-hee! So you let 'em have it?

HJALMAR: Right between the eyes.

EKDAL: Hear that, Gina? He let 'em have it right between the eyes of all the chamberlains.

GINA: Imagine that! Right between their eyes!

HJALMAR: Yes, but keep quiet about it. You don't want to talk about such things. Everything was very friendly, of course. They were all pleasant, genial people. I wouldn't want to hurt their feelings. That's not my way!

EKDAL: Right between their eyes, though—!

HEDVIG: *(caressingly)* It's so nice to see you in dress clothes! They really look good on you, daddy.

HJALMAR: That's true, isn't it? And this suit really fits me perfectly. Almost as if it was made to order— a little loose in the armpits maybe.... Help me, Hedvig. *(takes off the coat)* I think I'll put on my smoking jacket. Where did you put my jacket, Gina?

GINA: Here it is. *(brings the jacket and helps him)*

HJALMAR: That's better! Don't forget to give the coat back to Molvik first thing in the morning.

GINA: *(laying it away)* I'll take care of it.

HJALMAR: *(stretching himself)* This is much more comfy. An easy coat like this is more my style. Don't you think so, Hedvig?

43

HEDVIG: Yes, daddy.

HJALMAR: Especially if I tie my scarf like this—so it flows?

HEDVIG: Yes, it really goes with your mustache and your curly hair.

HJALMAR: I wouldn't say curly. My hair is wavy.

HEDVIG: Yes, you have beautiful curls.

HJALMAR: That's the word—wavy.

HEDVIG: *(after a pause, pulling his coat)* Daddy!

HJALMAR: Well, what do you want?

HEDVIG: You know what I want.

HJALMAR: I really don't.

HEDVIG: *(half laughing, half whispering)* Stop teasing me, daddy!

HJALMAR: Well, what is it?

HEDVIG: *(shaking him)* Stop pretending. Where are all the good things you promised me, daddy?

HJALMAR: Oh my—I completely forgot!

HEDVIG: You're only teasing me, daddy! Oh, you're so wicked! Where did you put them?

HJALMAR: No, it's true, I completely forgot. But wait a minute! I've got something else for you.

(Hedvig goes and searches in the pockets of the coat.)

HEDVIG: *(skipping and clapping her hands)* Oh mama, mama!

GINA: There, you see. If you just give him enough time—

HJALMAR: *(with a paper)* Look, here it is.

HEDVIG: That? It's just a piece of paper.

HJALMAR: This is the menu, my dear, the whole menu. See what it says? Bill of fare—that means menu.

HEDVIG: You don't have anything else?

HJALMAR: I told you I forgot the other stuff. But you can take my word for it, the food was really terrific. Sit down here and read the bill of fare while I tell you how everything tasted. Look, Hedvig.

HEDVIG: *(suppressing her tears)* Thank you. *(She seats herself, but does not read. Gina makes signs to her; Hjalmar notices.)*

HJALMAR: *(pacing up and down the room)* It's really incredible the kind of stuff the head of a family is expected to remember. And if he forgets the slightest thing, what does he get? Sour faces. Well, well, you get used to that after a while. *(stops near the stove, by the old man's chair)* Did you look in there tonight, father?

EKDAL: Of course. She's gone into the basket.

HJALMAR: Oh, she's in the basket. Then she's starting to get used to it.

EKDAL: Yes, I told you she would. But you know there are still a few small things—

HJALMAR: A few improvements, yes?

EKDAL: That have to be made, you know.

HJALMAR: Yes, let's talk about the improvements, father. Come sit on the couch.

EKDAL: I will. But I think I'll just fill my pipe first. It needs a cleaning too. *(he goes into his room)*

45

GINA: *(smiling to Hjalmar)* Cleaning his pipe!

HJALMAR: Come on, Gina, leave him alone—poor old shipwrecked man— Yes, those improvements — We'd better deal with them tomorrow.

GINA: Tomorrow you won't have time, Hjalmar.

HEDVIG: *(interposing)* Sure he will, mother!

GINA: Don't forget those prints have to be re-touched. They keep on asking for them.

HJALMAR: Well, well, those prints again! I'll finish them all right! Are there any new orders?

GINA: No, I'm sorry to say. We only have those two sittings tomorrow.

HJALMAR: That's all? Well, if people don't go to a little trouble—

GINA: What more can I do? I advertise in the news-paper as much as I can.

HJALMAR: The papers, the papers, you see how much good they do. And I suppose no one has looked at the room either?

GINA: No, not yet.

HJALMAR: Just what I expected. If people don't keep their eyes open—. You can't accomplish anything without real effort, Gina!

HEDVIG: *(going toward him)* Do you want your re-corder, daddy?

HJALMAR: No, no. There's no room for pleasures in my life. *(pacing about)* Yes, I'll work tomorrow, you'll see. I'll keep working as long as my strength holds out.

GINA: My dear good Ekdal, I didn't mean it that way.

HEDVIG: Can I bring you a bottle of beer, daddy?

HJALMAR: Absolutely not. I want nothing, nothing. *(comes to a standstill)* Did you say beer?

HEDVIG: *(cheerfully)* Yes, daddy, beautiful cold beer.

HJALMAR: Well, you can bring me a bottle, if you insist.

GINA: Yes, do that Hedvig. Then we'll be nice and cozy. *(Hedvig runs toward the kitchen door)*

HJALMAR: *(by the stove, stops her, looks at her, puts his arm round her neck and presses her to him)* Hedvig, Hedvig!

HEDVIG: *(with tears of joy)* My dear, sweet father!

HJALMAR: Don't say that. Here I've been gorging at a rich man's table—stuffing myself with food—! And I didn't even—!

GINA: *(sitting at the table)* That's silly, Ekdal.

HJALMAR: It's not silly! But don't be too hard on me. You know how much I love you anyway.

HEDVIG: *(throwing her arms round him)* And we love you, so much, daddy!

HJALMAR: And if sometimes I'm a little unreasonable—well, you'll remember, won't you, that I'm beset by a host of cares. There, there! *(dries his eyes)* We won't have beer at a time like this. Get me the recorder.

(Hedvig runs to the bookcase and fetches it.)

HJALMAR: Thank you! That's better. With my recorder in my hand and you two at my side—!

(Hedvig seats herself at the table near Gina. Hjalmar paces backward and forward, pipes up vigorously, and plays a Bohemian peasant dance, but in a slow plaintive tempo and with sentimental expression.)

HJALMAR: *(breaking off the melody, holds out his left hand to Gina, and says with emotion)* This place may be poor and humble, Gina, but it's home. And I say this with all my heart: here lies my happiness. *(he begins to play again; almost immediately after, a knocking is heard at the entrance door)*

GINA: *(rising)* Quiet, Hjalmar—I think there's someone at the door.

HJALMAR: *(laying the flute on the bookcase)* It figures! *(Gina goes and opens the door)*

GREGERS WERLE: *(in the passage)* Pardon me—

GINA: *(starting back slightly)* Oh!

GREGERS: —does Hjalmar Ekdal, the photographer, live here?

GINA: Yes, he does.

HJALMAR: *(going toward the door)* Gregers! It's you after all?

GREGERS: *(coming in)* I told you I'd come to see you.

HJALMAR: But tonight—? Did you leave the dinner?

GREGERS: I have left the dinner and my father's house, both. Good evening, Mrs. Ekdal, I don't know if you remember me?

GINA: Of course I do. It's not hard to remember young Mr. Werle.

GREGERS: No, I am very like my mother, and no doubt you remember her.

48

HJALMAR: You say you left your father's house?

GREGERS: Yes, I've moved to a hotel.

HJALMAR: Is that right? Well, since you're here, come in, come in, take off your coat and sit down.

GREGERS: Thanks. *(He takes off his overcoat. He is now dressed in a plain grey suit cut in a simple country manner.)*

HJALMAR: Sit on the couch. Make yourself comfortable. *(Gregers seats himself on the couch; Hjalmar takes a chair at the table)*

GREGERS: *(looking around him)* So this is where you live, Hjalmar. Is this where you work too?

HJALMAR: This is my studio, as you can see—

GINA: It's our largest room, so we usually sit here.

HJALMAR. We used to have a better place. But this has one big advantage. There's a lot of space.

GINA: And there's a room across the hall which we can rent.

GREGERS: *(to Hjalmar)* Ah, so you keep lodgers here?

HJALMAR: No, not yet. They're not so easy to find. You have to keep your eyes open. What about that beer now? *(Hedvig nods and goes out into the kitchen)*

GREGERS: So that's your daughter?

HJALMAR: Yes, that's Hedvig.

GREGERS: And she's your only child?

HJALMAR: Yes, our only child. The joy of our lives, and— *(lowering his voice)* also our deepest sorrow, Gregers.

GREGERS: What do you mean?

HJALMAR: She's in serious danger of losing her sight.

GREGERS: Going blind?

HJALMAR: Yes. She has only the early symptoms, and it may not hit her for a while. But the doctor has warned us it's inevitable.

GREGERS: What a terrible thing!

HJALMAR: *(sighs)* It's hereditary.

GINA: Hjalmar's mother had weak eyes.

HJALMAR: So my father says, but I can't remember her.

GREGERS: Poor child! And how does she deal with it?

HJALMAR: Oh, you can understand we haven't the heart to tell her yet. She has no suspicion. She's gay and carefree as a little bird, fluttering forward into a life of endless night. *(overcome)* Oh, it's so hard on me, Gregers.

(Hedvig brings a tray with beer and glasses, which she sets on the table.)

HJALMAR: *(stroking her hair)* Thank you, thank you, Hedvig. *(Hedvig puts her arm round his neck and whispers in his ear)* No, forget the bread and butter for now. *(looks up)* Unless you would like some, Gregers?

GREGERS: *(with a gesture of refusal)* No, thank you.

HJALMAR: *(still melancholy)* Well, you might as well bring in a little. Just a crust, that's all I want. And put plenty of butter on it.

(Hedvig nods gaily and goes out into the kitchen again.)

GREGERS: *(who had been following her with his eyes)* She seems pretty healthy otherwise.

GINA: Yes. She's perfectly sound in all other respects, thank heaven.

GREGERS: She's growing to look very much like you, Mrs. Ekdal. How old is she now?

GINA: Almost fourteen. She has a birthday day after tomorrow.

GREGERS: She's tall for her age.

GINA: Yes, she shot up wonderful this last year.

GREGERS: These young people growing up make you feel the years. How long have you been married now?

GINA: We've been married—let's see—going on fifteen years.

GREGERS: That long?

GINA: *(watches him carefully)* Yes, that long.

HJALMAR: Yes, fifteen years minus a few months. *(changing his tone)* They must have seemed long years for you, Gregers, living up at the mill.

GREGERS: They did seem long—getting through them. But now they're over, I can't believe how fast the time has passed.

(Old Ekdal comes from his room without his pipe, but with his old-fashioned uniform cap on his head, walking a little unsteadily.)

EKDAL: Hjalmar, now we can sit and have a good talk about the—hm—what were we going to talk about?

HJALMAR: *(going toward him)* Father, we have someone

here—Gregers Werle. I don't know if you remember him.

EKDAL: *(looking at Gregers, who has risen)* Werle? You mean the son? What does he want with me?

HJALMAR: Nothing. He's here to see me.

EKDAL: Oh! Then nothing's wrong?

HJALMAR: No, no, of course not.

EKDAL: *(with a large gesture)* Not that I'm afraid, you know, but—

GREGERS: *(goes over to him)* I bring you greetings from your old hunting grounds, Lieutenant Ekdal.

EKDAL: Hunting grounds?

GREGERS: Yes, up in Hoidal.

EKDAL: Oh, up there. Yes, I was very well known up there once upon a time.

GREGERS: You were a great hunter then.

EKDAL: Yes, I was, I don't deny it. You're looking at my cap. I don't ask anyone's permission to wear it in the house. As long as I don't wear it out in the street—

(Hedvig brings a plate of bread and butter, which she sets on the table.)

HJALMAR: Sit down, father, and have some beer. Help yourself, Gregers.

(Ekdal mutters and stumbles over to the sofa. Gregers seats himself on the chair nearest to him, Hjalmar on the other side of Gregers. Gina sits a little way from the table, sewing; Hedvig stands beside her father.)

GREGERS: Do you remember, Lieutenant Ekdal, how

52

Hjalmar and I used to come and visit you in the summer and during Christmas?

EKDAL: You did? No, no, no, I don't remember that. But I was certainly a good hunter in my day. I shot bears too. Nine of them I shot.

GREGERS: *(looking sympathetically at him)* And now you don't hunt anymore?

EKDAL: I wouldn't say that, sir. I get off a shot now and then. Not in the old way, of course. In the woods you know—the woods, the woods—! *(drinks)* What are the woods like up there now?

GREGERS: Not as good as in your day. A lot has been cut down.

EKDAL: Cut down? *(more softly, and as if afraid)* That's a dangerous thing to do. That'll bring bad things. The woods will have their revenge.

HJALMAR: *(filling up his glass)* Have a little more, father.

GREGERS: How can a man like you—someone so used to the open air—how can you live in such a stuffy town, boxed in by four walls?

EKDAL: *(laughs quietly and glances at Hjalmar)* Oh, it's not so bad here. Not bad at all.

GREGERS: But you don't miss all the things you had—the cool fresh breezes, the free life in the woods and on the moors, among the beasts and the birds—?

EKDAL: *(smiling)* Hjalmar, shall we show it to him?

HJALMAR: *(hastily and a little embarrassed)* No no, father, not tonight.

GREGERS: What does he want to show me?

53

HJALMAR: Oh, it's only a kind of—you'll see it some other time.

GREGERS: *(continues, to the old man)* What I was thinking, Lieutenant Ekdal, was that you should come back with me to the mill. I'm going up there very soon. You could get some copying to do there too. And here, there's nothing to interest you— nothing to cheer you up.

EKDAL: *(stares in astonishment at him)* There's nothing here to—!

GREGERS: Well, it's true you have Hjalmar. But then he has his own family. For a man like you, who's always been so passionate about what's free and wild—

EKDAL: *(thumps the table)* Hjalmar, he's going to see it!

HJALMAR: But, father, do you think it's worth it? It's dark now, you know.

EKDAL: Nonsense, there's a moon. *(rises)* He's going to see it, I tell you. Let me go! And come and help me, Hjalmar.

HEDVIG: Yes, daddy, do!

HJALMAR: *(rising)* All right then.

GREGERS: *(to Gina)* What do they want me to see?

GINA: Oh, don't think you're gonna see anything real special.

(Ekdal and Hjalmar have gone to the back wall and are each pushing back a side of the sliding door. Hedvig helps the old man. Gregers remains standing by the sofa. Gina sits still and sews. Through the open doorway a large, deep, irregular attic is seen with odd nooks and corners, a couple of stovepipes running

*through it from rooms below. There are skylights through
which clear moonbeams shine in on some parts of the
great room; others lie in deep shadow.)*

EKDAL: *(to Gregers)* You can get a little closer, if you
want.

GREGERS: *(going over to them)* Well, what is it?

EKDAL: See for yourself. Hm.

HJALMAR: *(somewhat embarrassed)* This is all my father's, you know.

GREGERS: *(at the door, looks into the garret)* What, you
keep chickens here, Lieutenant Ekdal?

EKDAL: Do we keep chickens! They're roosting now.
But wait till you see them in the daytime, sir!

HEDVIG: And we have a—

EKDAL: Sh! Nothing about that yet.

GREGERS: You've got pigeons too, I see.

EKDAL: Oh yes, have we got pigeons! They have their
nesting boxes just there. Pigeons like to nest
high, you know.

GREGERS: These aren't like common pigeons.

EKDAL: Common! Well, I guess not! We got tum-
blers, and a pair of pouters too. But come over
here! Do you see that hutch down there by the
wall?

GREGERS: Yes. What's it for?

EKDAL: That's where the rabbits sleep, sir.

GREGERS: You mean you have rabbits too?

EKDAL: Have we got rabbits! He wants to know if we

got rabbits, Hjalmar! Hm! But now comes the big attraction! Here we have it! Out of the way, Hedvig. Stand here, that's it. And now look there. Do you see a basket with straw in it?

GREGERS: Yes. And there's a bird lying in the basket.

EKDAL: Hm—"a bird."

GREGERS: Is it a duck?

EKDAL: *(hurt)* Of course it's a duck.

HJALMAR: But what kind of duck?

HEDVIG: It's not just an ordinary duck—

EKDAL: Sh!

GREGERS: And it's not a Muscovy duck either?

EKDAL: No, Mr.—Werle, it's not a Muscovy duck. It's a wild duck!

GREGERS: Really? A wild duck?

EKDAL: That's what it is. That "bird" as you call it is a wild duck. Our wild duck, sir.

HEDVIG: My wild duck. She belongs to me.

GREGERS: And can it live up here in the garret? How does it survive?

EKDAL: She has a trough of water to splash around in, you know.

HJALMAR: Fresh water every other day.

GINA: *(turning toward Hjalmar)* Hjalmar, dear, this place is getting ice cold.

EKDAL: Hm, we'd better close up then. It's not good to disturb their night's rest. Close up, Hedvig.

(Hjalmar and Hedvig push the garret doors together.)

56

EKDAL: Some other time you get to see her proper *(seats himself in the armchair by the stove)* Oh, they're strange things, those wild ducks, I can tell you.

GREGERS: How did you manage to catch it, Lieutenant Ekdal?

EKDAL: I didn't catch her. There's a certain man around here who we have to thank for her.

GREGERS: *(starts slightly)* You're not talking about my father, are you?

EKDAL: That's right. Your father and no one else. Hm.

HJALMAR: How did you guess that, Gregers?

GREGERS: You told me how much you owed my father for so many things. So I thought—

GINA: But we didn't get the duck from Mr. Werle himself—

EKDAL: Still, it's Haakon Werle who we have to thank for her, Gina. *(to Gregers)* He was hunting from a boat, and he brought her down. But your father can't see very well now. Hm. He only wounded her.

GREGERS: Ah! She took a couple of slugs in her body, I would guess.

HJALMAR: Yes, two or three.

HEDVIG: She got hit under the wing, so she couldn't fly.

GREGERS: And so she dove to the bottom, right?

EKDAL: *(sleepily, in a thick voice)* Naturally. Wild ducks always do that. They shoot to the bottom as deep as they can get, sir—and tangle themselves in the

57

muck and seaweed—and all the garbage down there. And they never come up again.

GREGERS: But your wild duck came up again, Lieutenant Ekdal.

EKDAL: He had a very clever dog, your father did. And that dog—he dove down after the duck and brought her up again.

GREGERS: *(who has turned to Hjalmar)* And then you got her?

HJALMAR: Not right away. First your father took her home. But she didn't thrive there. So he asked Peterson to put her to sleep—

EKDAL: *(half asleep)* Hm—yes—Peterson—that asshole—

HJALMAR: *(speaking more softly)* That was how we got her, you see. Father knows Peterson a little. And when he heard about the wild duck he asked him to give her to us.

GREGERS: And now she's doing well in the storeroom?

HJALMAR: Yes, very well. She's gotten fat. You see, she's lived in there so long now that she's forgotten all about her past wild life, and that's all she needed.

GREGERS: You're right there, Hjalmar. Only don't let her ever see the sky and the water— . But I won't stay any longer. I think your father has gone to sleep.

HJALMAR: Oh, don't go because of that—

GREGERS: By the way—you said you had a room for rent—a spare room?

HJALMAR: Yes—why? Do you know anybody who—?

GREGERS: Can I have the room?

HJALMAR: You want it?

GINA: Oh no, Mr. Werle, you don't want—

GREGERS: Can I have the room? If you say yes, I'll move in first thing in the morning.

HJALMAR: Certainly, with great pleasure—

GINA: Mr. Werle, I don't think it's anywhere near the right sort of room for you.

HJALMAR: Gina! How can you say that?

GINA: It's not big enough or light enough, or—

GREGERS: That really doesn't matter, Mrs. Ekdal.

HJALMAR: It think it's a very nice room, and not badly furnished either.

GINA: But don't forget those two on the first floor.

GREGERS: What two?

GINA: Well, one used to be a theologist or something like that—

HJALMAR: That's Molvik—er, *Mr.* Molvik. He has a degree.

GINA: And the other's a doctor, named Relling.

GREGERS: Relling? I know him a little. He used to practice up at Hoidal.

GINA: They're a pair of lowlifes. They're often out on the town at night, and they come home at all hours, and not always—

GREGERS: I'll get used to that pretty quick. I hope to settle in just like the wild duck—

GINA: Well, I think you should sleep on it first, anyway.

GREGERS: You don't seem very happy about having me in the house, Mrs. Ekdal.

GINA: Oh, no! Why do you say that?

HJALMAR: Well, you are behaving a little strangely, Gina. *(to Gregers)* So you're planning to stay in town for a while?

GREGERS: *(putting on his overcoat)* Yes, I am going to stay here.

HJALMAR: But not with your father? What do you intend to do, then?

GREGERS: If I knew that, Hjalmar, everything would be clear! But when one has the misfortune to be called Gregers—"Gregers"!—followed by "Werle." Did you ever hear anything so ugly?

HJALMAR: Oh, it doesn't sound bad at all.

GREGERS: I'd be tempted to spit on any man who answered to a name like that. Once you're doomed to live with the name Gregers Werle, like me—

HJALMAR: *(laughs)* Ha, ha! If you weren't Gregers Werle, what would you like to be?

GREGERS: If I had my choice, I'd be a dog.

GINA: A dog!

HEDVIG: *(involuntarily)* Oh, no!

GREGERS: Yes, an extremely clever dog, one that dives to the bottom after wild ducks when they grab fast in muck and seaweed, down in the ooze.

HJALMAR: I have to admit, Gregers, I haven't a clue what you're talking about.

GREGERS: And you wouldn't be any wiser if you did. So it's settled, then. I move in early tomorrow morning. *(to Gina)* I won't cause you any trouble. I can take care of myself. *(to Hjalmar)* We'll finish our talk tomorrow. Good night, Mrs. Ekdal. *(nods to Hedvig)* Good night.

GINA: Good night, Mr. Werle.

HEDVIG: Good night.

HJALMAR: *(who has lighted a candle)* Wait a moment, I'll light the way. The stairs are sure to be dark. *(Gregers and Hjalmar go out by the passage door)*

GINA: *(looking straight before her, with her sewing in her lap)* Wasn't that peculiar what he said about wanting to be a dog?

HEDVIG: You know, mother, I think he meant something very different by that.

GINA: What else could he mean?

HEDVIG: I don't know. But I thought he meant something different from what he was saying—all the time.

GINA: Do you think so? He certainly was peculiar.

HJALMAR: *(comes back)* Now, at last, I can get a mouthful of food. *(begins to eat the bread and butter)* Well, you see, Gina—if you just keep your eyes open—

GINA: What do you mean, keep your eyes open—?

HJALMAR: Well, aren't we lucky to get the room rented? And to such a man as Gregers—such a good old friend.

GINA: Well, I really don't know what to say about it.

HEDVIG: Oh, mother, you'll see. It'll be fun!

HJALMAR: You're really strange. Before you were so eager to rent the room, and now you're not happy.

GINA: Yes I am, Ekdal. But if only it was to someone else. What do you suppose his father will say?

HJALMAR: Old Werle? It's none of his business.

GINA: But you must see that something is happening between them again, or he wouldn't be leaving his father's house. You know those two don't get along.

HJALMAR: That's possible, but—

GINA: And now Mr. Werle will think it's you egged him on—

HJALMAR: Let him think so, then! I won't deny that Mr. Werle has done a lot for me. But that doesn't make me his slave for life.

GINA: But Ekdal, grandfather might have to suffer for it. He may lose the little bit of work he gets from Graberg.

HJALMAR: So much the better! Don't you find it humiliating for someone like me to see his grey-haired old father treated like an outcast? But now I think things are turning around. *(takes a fresh piece of bread and butter)* I have a purpose in life, and I aim to fulfill it!

HEDVIG: Oh yes, father, do!

GINA: Sh! Don't wake him!

HJALMAR: *(more softly)* I *will* fulfill it, I tell you. The day will come when—when—and that's why it's good we rented the room. It makes me more independent. A man with a purpose in life must be independent. *(by the armchair, with emotion)* Poor old grey-haired father! You can depend on your Hjalmar. He has broad shoulders—strong shoulders, at any rate. You'll wake up some fine day and— *(to Gina)* You don't believe it?

GINA: *(rising)* Of course I do. But let's start by putting him to bed.

HJALMAR: Yes, let's put him to bed. *(they take hold of the old man carefully)*

ACT 3

Hjalmar Ekdal's studio. It is morning: the daylight shines through the large slanting skylight; the curtain is drawn back.

Hjalmar is sitting at the table, busy retouching a photograph. Several others lie before him. Soon Gina, wearing a hat and cloak, enters by the outer door. She has a covered basket on her arm.

HJALMAR: Back already, Gina?

GINA: Oh yes, there's no time to waste. *(sets her basket on a chair and takes off her things)*

HJALMAR: Did you get a look at Greger's room?

GINA: I sure did, and it's something to see, I can tell you. He made a mess of it as soon as he arrived.

HJALMAR: How?

GINA: He had to do everything himself, he said. So he tries to light the stove, and what happens but he screws down the damper so the whole room is filled with smoke. Pew! What a stink—

HJALMAR: You're kidding me!

GINA: But you haven't heard the worst of it. He has to put out the fire, right? So he pours his wash water onto the stove and makes the whole floor one filthy mess.

HJALMAR: What a nuisance!

GINA: I've got the porter's wife to clean up after him, the pig! But the room won't be livable until afternoon.

HJALMAR: What's he doing in the meantime?

GINA: Said he was going out for a bit.

HJALMAR: I looked in on him too, for a minute—after you left.

GINA: So he told me. You've asked him up for lunch.

HJALMAR: Just for a bite, you know. It's his first day in the house—we couldn't do less. You have something to eat, I suppose?

GINA: I'll see what I can turn up.

HJALMAR: Don't scrimp, because I think Relling and Molvik are coming too. I just happened to meet Relling on the stairs, you see, so I had to—

GINA: We got to feed those two as well?

HJALMAR: For heaven's sake—one or two more or less won't make any difference.

OLD EKDAL: *(opens his door and looks in)* Look, Hjalmar— *(sees Gina)* Oh!

GINA: Do you want something, grandfather?

EKDAL: No, no, it doesn't matter. Hm! *(retires again)*

GINA: *(takes up the basket)* Make sure he doesn't go out.

HJALMAR: All right, all right. And Gina, a little herring salad would be nice. Relling and Molvik were out on the town again last night.

GINA: As long as they don't come up before I'm ready for them—

65

HJALMAR: They won't. Take your time.

GINA: That's good. And meanwhile you could do a little work.

HJALMAR: I am working! I'm working as hard as I can!

GINA: Then you'll be done with it. *(She goes out to the kitchen with her basket. Hjalmar sits for a time, penciling away at the photograph in an indolent and listless manner.)*

EKDAL: *(peeps in, looks round the studio, and says softly)* Are you working?

HJALMAR: Yes, I'm working on these portraits—

EKDAL: Well, well, it doesn't matter—since you're so busy—hm! *(he goes out again; the door stands open)*

HJALMAR: *(continues for some time in silence, then lays down his brush and goes over to the door)* Are you working, father?

EKDAL: *(in a grumbling tone, within)* If you're working, I'm working. Hm!

HJALMAR: Oh, all right, then. *(goes to his work again)*

EKDAL: *(presently, coming to the door again)* Hm. Hjalmar, you know I'm not working all that hard.

HJALMAR: I thought you were doing some copying.

EKDAL: To hell with it! Can't Graberg wait a day or two? After all, it's not a matter of life and death.

HJALMAR: No, and you're not his slave either.

EKDAL: And there's that other thing down there—

HJALMAR: You read my mind. Do you want to go in? Do you want me to open the door for you?

66

EKDAL: Not such a bad idea.

HJALMAR: *(rises)* Then we'll be done with it.

EKDAL: That's right, yes. It has to be ready first thing tomorrow. We did say tomorrow, didn't we? Hm?

HJALMAR: Yes, we said tomorrow.

(Hjalmar and Ekdal each push aside half of the sliding door. The morning sun is shining in through the skylight. Some doves are flying about; others sit cooing on their perches. The hens are occasionally heard clucking, farther back in the attic.)

HJALMAR: There—now you can get to work, father.

EKDAL: *(goes in)* Aren't you coming?

HJALMAR: Well, I'm not sure—I kind of think— *(sees Gina at the kitchen door)* No, I don't have time; I have to work. *(goes to the table)* There! Now maybe I can have a little peace.

GINA: Is he rummaging around down there again?

HJALMAR: Would you rather he went to Mrs. Ericson's? *(seats himself)* You want something? You look like—

GINA: I only wanted to ask if you thought we could eat lunch here?

HJALMAR: Yes, we have no one coming to sit this early, do we?

GINA: There's no one today but that couple who want to be photographed together.

HJALMAR: Why the hell couldn't they choose another day!

GINA: They're coming in the afternoon, dear Ekdal, when you're taking your nap.

HJALMAR: All right, let's have lunch here then.

GINA: Fine, but there's no great rush laying the table-cloth. You can still use the table for a good while yet.

HJALMAR: You think I'm not working hard enough? I use the table as much as I can!

GINA: Then you'll have some free time later, you know. *(goes out into the kitchen again; short pause)*

EKDAL: *(in the attic doorway, behind the net)* Hjalmar!

HJALMAR: Well?

EKDAL: I'm afraid we'll have to move the water trough, after all.

HJALMAR: What have I been saying all along?

EKDAL: Hm—hm—hm. *(Goes away from the door again. Hjalmar goes on working a little; glances toward the attic and half rises. Hedvig comes in from the kitchen.)*

HJALMAR: *(sits down again hurriedly)* What do you want?

HEDVIG: I only wanted to be near you, daddy.

HJALMAR: *(after a pause)* Why are you poking around like that? Did someone tell you to keep an eye on me?

HEDVIG: No, no.

HJALMAR: What is your mother up to in there?

HEDVIG: She's making the herring salad. *(goes to the table)* Is there anything I could help you with, daddy?

HJALMAR: Oh, no. It's my fate to bear the whole burden—assuming my strength holds out. You don't

68

have to worry about helping me, Hedvig—as long as I have my health.

HEDVIG: Oh, daddy! Don't say those awful things. *(she wanders about a little, stops by the doorway, and looks into the attic)*

HJALMAR: Tell me, what's he up to?

HEDVIG: I think he's building a new path to the water trough.

HJALMAR: He can't do that by himself! And I have to sit here and—!

HEDVIG: *(goes to him)* Give me the brush, daddy. I can do it perfectly well.

HJALMAR: Nonsense. You'll just strain your eyes.

HEDVIG: Don't worry. I'm all right. Give me the brush.

HJALMAR: *(rising)* Well, it won't take me more than a minute or two.

HEDVIG: Pooh, so what's the harm? *(takes the brush)* Now then! *(seats herself)* I can use this one as a model.

HJALMAR: But don't hurt your eyes, do you hear? I won't be responsible. You're responsible, understand?

HEDVIG: *(retouching)* Yes, yes, I understand.

HJALMAR: You're pretty good at it, Hedvig. Just a minute or two, you know. *(He slips through by the edge of the curtain into the attic. Hedvig sits at her work. Hjalmar and Ekdal are heard discussing something inside.)*

HJALMAR: *(appears behind the net)* Hedvig, hand me those pliers on the shelf. And also the hammer.

69

(turns away inside) Now I'll show you, father. Here's what I mean!

(Hedvig has brought the requested tools from the shelf, and hands them to him through the net.)

HJALMAR: Ah, thanks. It's lucky I came in.

(Goes back from the curtain again; they are heard carpentering and talking inside. Hedvig stands looking in at them. A moment later there is a knock at the passage door; she does not notice it.)

GREGERS WERLE: *(bareheaded, without an overcoat, enters and stops near the door)* Ahem!

HEDVIG: *(turns and goes toward him)* Good morning. Please come in.

GREGERS: Thank you. *(looking toward the attic)* You seem to have workmen in the house.

HEDVIG: No, it is only father and grandfather. I'll tell them you're here.

GREGERS: Don't do that. I'd rather wait a little. *(seats himself on the sofa)*

HEDVIG: It's so messy here— *(begins to clear away the photographs)*

GREGERS: Oh, leave those. Are these the prints that have to be finished?

HEDVIG: Yes, I was helping my father with them.

GREGERS: Please don't let me disturb you.

HEDVIG: Oh, you don't. *(she gathers the things to her and sits down to work; Gregers looks at her, meanwhile, in silence)*

GREGERS: Did the wild duck sleep well last night?

HEDVIG: Yes, I think so, thanks.

70

GREGERS: *(turning toward the attic)* In the daytime it looks different than in the moonlight.

HEDVIG: Yes, it changes with the time of day. It looks different in the morning than the evening; and it's different when it's sunny or raining.

GREGERS: You've noticed that?

HEDVIG: Difficult not to.

GREGERS: Are you also fond of being in there with the wild duck?

HEDVIG: Yes, when I have the time—

GREGERS: I suppose you don't have much time. You go to school, don't you?

HEDVIG: Not any more. My father's afraid I'll hurt my eyes.

GREGERS: Oh, then he reads with you himself?

HEDVIG: Daddy has promised to read with me, but he hasn't had the time yet.

GREGERS: Is there nobody else to help you a little?

HEDVIG: There's Mr. Molvik. But he's not always exactly—not always quite—

GREGERS: Sober?

HEDVIG: You might say that!

GREGERS: Then you have a lot of time on your hands. And I suppose it's a whole little world in there?

HEDVIG: That's right. And it's full of peculiar things.

GREGERS: Really?

HEDVIG: There are big closets full of books. And a lot of the books have pictures in them.

GREGERS: I see.

HEDVIG: And then there's an old desk with drawers and flaps, and a big clock with figures that go in and out when the clock strikes. But it isn't working now.

GREGERS: So time has come to a stop in there—in the world of the wild duck.

HEDVIG: Yes. And there's an old paintbox and things —and all the books.

GREGERS: And you enjoy reading the books?

HEDVIG: Oh yes, when I get the chance. Most of them are written in a foreign language though, and I don't know foreign languages. But I can always look at the pictures. There's one really big book called "Harrison's History of London." It must be a hundred years old, and there are a whole lot of pictures in it. In the front there's a picture of Death with an hourglass, and a young woman. I don't like that at all. But then there are all the other pictures of churches, and castles, and streets, and big ships sailing on the sea.

GREGERS: But where did all those wonderful things come from?

HEDVIG: An old sea captain once lived there, and he would bring them home with him. They called him "The Flying Dutchman." That was kind of peculiar, because he wasn't a Dutchman at all.

GREGERS: He wasn't?

HEDVIG: No. But he never returned, and left all those things here.

GREGERS: Tell me something. When you're sitting in

there looking at the pictures, don't you ever want to get out and see the real world for yourself?

HEDVIG: Oh, no! I want to stay home and help my father and mother.

GREGERS: Retouching photographs?

HEDVIG: Not just that. What I want more than anything is to learn to engrave pictures like those in the foreign books.

GREGERS: Hm. And what does your father say about that?

HEDVIG: I don't think he likes it. My father is peculiar about things like that. He wants me to do odd things like basket-weaving and wicker work! I don't see much use in that.

GREGERS: Me neither.

HEDVIG: But my father was right to say that if I'd learned basket-weaving I could have made the wild duck's new basket.

GREGERS: Yes you could've. And that was really your job, wasn't it?

HEDVIG: Yes, because it's my wild duck.

GREGERS: Of course it is.

HEDVIG: Yes, she belongs to me. But I lend her to my father and grandfather whenever they want.

GREGERS: I see. But what do they want with her?

HEDVIG: Well, they care for her, and build places for her, and things like that.

GREGERS: I see. So the wild duck is the most important creature in the storeroom?

HEDVIG: She certainly is. She's a real wild duck, you know. But poor thing, she has no one to turn to.

GREGERS: No brothers and sisters, like rabbits have—

HEDVIG: No. The hens, most of them, were little chicks together. But she was taken away from all her kind. It's a real mystery about the wild duck. No one knows her, and nobody knows where she came from.

GREGERS: And she's been down in the depths of the sea.

HEDVIG: *(with a quick glance at him, represses a smile and asks)* Why do you call it "depths of the sea"?

GREGERS: What else should I call it?

HEDVIG: You might have said "the bottom of the sea."

GREGERS: Isn't that the same as "the depths of the sea"?

HEDVIG: Yes. But it sounds so peculiar when other people talk about the depths of the sea.

GREGERS: Really? Why?

HEDVIG: I can't. It's too silly.

GREGERS: No it's not. Tell me why you smiled.

HEDVIG: Well, whenever I suddenly think about what's in there, it seems to me that the whole room and everything in it is called "the depths of the sea." But that's so silly.

GREGERS: Don't say that.

HEDVIG: Well, it's only a storeroom, you know.

GREGERS: *(looks fixedly at her)* Are you so sure of that?

HEDVIG: *(astonished)* That it's a storeroom?

GREGERS: Are you so sure of that?

(Hedvig is silent and looks at him open-mouthed. Gina comes in from the kitchen with the table things.)

GREGERS: *(rising)* I'm afraid I've come too early.

GINA: Oh, you have to put yourself somewhere. And lunch is nearly ready now, anyway. Clear the table, Hedvig.

(Hedvig clears away her things. She and Gina lay the tablecloth during what follows. Gregers seats himself in the armchair and turns over an album.)

GREGERS: I hear you do retouching, Mrs. Ekdal.

GINA: *(with a side glance)* Yes, I do.

GREGERS: That was really lucky.

GINA: Why lucky?

GREGERS: I mean because Ekdal took up photography.

HEDVIG: My mother can take photographs too.

GINA: Oh yes. I had to learn that.

GREGERS: So you're the one who runs the business then?

GINA: Yes, when Ekdal doesn't have the time—

GREGERS: He spends a lot of time with his old father, I guess.

GINA: Yes, and it's not good work for a man like Ekdal—taking stupid pictures all day long.

GREGERS: I agree with you there, but once he chose this line of work—

GINA: You have to understand, Mr. Werle, that Ekdal's not one of your everyday photographers.

GREGERS: Of course not, but still— *(a shot is fired from within the attic)*

GREGERS: *(starting up)* What's that?

GINA: Ugh! They're shooting again!

GREGERS: Do they have guns in there?

HEDVIG: They go out hunting.

GREGERS: In the storeroom? Are you shooting, Hjalmar?

HJALMAR: *(inside the net)* Is that you? I didn't know you were here. I was so busy— *(to Hedvig)* Why didn't you tell us? *(comes into the studio)*

GREGERS: Do you go hunting in the storeroom?

HJALMAR: *(showing a double-barreled pistol)* Only with this old thing.

GINA: You and grandfather will get yourselves in trouble one day with that there gun.

HJALMAR: *(with irritation)* I believe you've been told that this particular kind of firearm is called a pistol.

GINA: Well, that doesn't make it any better, does it?

GREGERS: So you've become a hunter too, Hjalmar?

HJALMAR: Only a rabbit or two once in a while. Mostly to please my father, you know.

GINA: Men are peculiar people. They always have to bemuse themselves.

HJALMAR: *(snappishly)* Yes, we always have to amuse ourselves.

GINA: That's just what I said.

HJALMAR: Hm. *(to Gregers)* You see, the storeroom is

in a place where no one can hear us shooting. *(lays the pistol on the top shelf of the bookcase)* Don't touch that pistol, Hedvig! One barrel is loaded, remember.

GREGERS: *(looking through the net)* You have a hunting rifle too, I see.

HJALMAR: That's my father's old gun. It's useless now. The lock is broken. But it's fun having it anyway. We can take it apart now and then, and clean it and oil it, and put it all together again. Of course, it's mostly my father who plays around with that sort of thing.

HEDVIG: *(beside Gregers)* Now you can see the wild duck clearly.

GREGERS: I was just looking at her. She's dragging a wing.

HEDVIG: Well, there's nothing peculiar about that. She was shot, you know.

GREGERS: And isn't she limping a little?

HJALMAR: Maybe a little.

HEDVIG: Yes, that's where the dog got ahold of her.

HJALMAR: But she's perfect in every other way. And that's really remarkable for a creature that's taken a charge of buckshot in her wing, that a dog has held in his teeth—

GREGERS: *(with a glance at Hedvig)* And that's been down so long in the depths of the sea.

HEDVIG: *(smiling)* Yes.

GINA: *(laying the table)* That blessed wild duck! What a fuss you make over her.

HJALMAR: Hm. When's lunch going to be ready?

GINA: Very soon. Come and help me, Hedvig. *(Gina and Hedvig go out into the kitchen)*

HJALMAR: *(in a low voice)* I don't think you'd better stand there looking at my father. It bothers him. *(Gregers moves away from the storeroom door)* I may as well shut the place up before the others come. *(claps his hands to drive the fowls back)* Shh—shh, get in with you! *(draws up the curtain and pulls the doors together)* That gadget is my own invention. It's really quite interesting to putter around with such things, to repair them when they get broken. It's also absolutely necessary. Gina doesn't like rabbits and fowls marching around the studio.

GREGERS: I can understand that. I suppose the studio is your wife's special department?

HJALMAR: The ordinary stuff I give to her. That way I can shut myself up in the sitting room and think about more important things.

GREGERS: What kind of things, Hjalmar?

HJALMAR: I'm surprised you haven't asked me that before. But maybe no one's told you about the invention?

GREGERS: The invention? No.

HJALMAR: Really? You haven't heard of it? Oh, of course, when you're up there in the wilderness—

GREGERS: So you've invented something?

HJALMAR: It's not exactly perfected yet, but I'm working on it. When I decided to devote myself to photography, you know, it wasn't just to take pictures of the hoi polloi.

GREGERS: That's what your wife was just saying.

HJALMAR: I swore that if I devoted my powers to this trade, I would have to elevate it into both an art and a science. That's why I decided to create this great invention.

GREGERS: But what kind of invention is it? What will it do?

HJALMAR: My dear fellow, don't ask me for details yet. It takes time, you know. And don't think I'm doing this for the sake of vanity. I don't do this work for myself. No, I am guided night and day by my purpose in life.

GREGERS: What is your purpose in life?

HJALMAR: Have you forgotten that old grey-haired man?

GREGERS: Your poor father? Yes, but what can you do for him?

HJALMAR: I can revive his self-respect, by restoring honor and dignity to the name of Ekdal.

GREGERS: So that's your purpose in life?

HJALMAR: Yes. I mean to rescue that shipwrecked man. For that's what he was—shipwrecked—when that storm hit him. The day those terrible investigations began, he was no longer himself. That pistol there—the one we shoot rabbits with—has played its role in the tragedy of the Ekdals.

GREGERS: That pistol? Really?

HJALMAR: After he was sentenced to prison, he had that pistol in his hand—

GREGERS: He did—?

HJALMAR: But he couldn't use it. His courage failed

him. So broken, so demoralized was he at the time! Can you imagine it? This man, a soldier, who had shot nine bears, who was descended from two lieutenant colonels—one after the other, of course. Can you understand it, Gregers?

GREGERS: Yes, I can understand it perfectly well.

HJALMAR: I can't. And there was another time that pistol played a part in the history of our house. When they put on his prison uniform and locked him up behind bars—oh, that was a terrible time for me, I can tell you. I pulled the blinds down over both my windows. When I peeped out, I saw the sun was shining as if nothing had happened. I couldn't imagine it. I saw people walking along the street, laughing and talking about meaningless things. I couldn't understand it. I thought the whole world must be standing still—like in an eclipse.

GREGERS: I felt that way when my mother died.

HJALMAR: It was in just such a time that Hjalmar Ekdal pointed that pistol at his own heart.

GREGERS: You also thought of—!

HJALMAR: Yes.

GREGERS: Why didn't you shoot?

HJALMAR: At the decisive moment I won a great victory over myself. I went on living. But I can tell you, it takes a lot of courage to choose life in the face of such circumstances.

GREGERS: Well, that all depends on how you look at it.

HJALMAR: Yes, a lot of courage. But I'm glad I was resolute, because now I will soon perfect my invention. And Dr. Relling thinks—and I agree with him—that my father should be allowed to wear his uniform again. That I will claim as my only reward.

GREGERS: So that's what he meant about his uniform—?

HJALMAR: Yes, that is his most coveted goal in life. You have no idea how my heart bleeds for him. Every time we celebrate an anniversary—Gina's and my wedding day, or whatever—in comes the old man dressed in the uniform he used to wear in happier days. But if he hears so much as a knock at the door—he doesn't dare show himself to strangers, you know—he hurries back into his room as fast as his old legs will carry him. Oh, it breaks a son's heart to witness such things!

GREGERS: How long do you figure it will take you to finish your invention?

HJALMAR: Come now, you mustn't expect me to reveal details like that. An inventor can't completely control his genius. Everything depends on inspiration—on intuition—and it's almost impossible to predict when that will come.

GREGERS: But you're making progress?

HJALMAR: Of course I'm making progress. Every day I turn it over in my mind. I'm possessed by it. Every afternoon, after I've had my dinner, I shut myself up in the living room, where I can reflect without being disturbed. But I can't be hurried. It doesn't do a bit of good. Relling says that too.

GREGERS: But don't you think all that stuff in the storeroom distracts your attention too much?

HJALMAR: Not a bit, not a bit. Just the opposite. Don't say that. I can't be constantly preoccupied with the same train of thought. I need something to think about while I'm waiting for inspiration. When it comes, it comes, and you can't force it.

GREGERS: Hjalmar, my friend, I'm beginning to think there's something of the wild duck in you.

HJALMAR: Something of the wild duck? What do you mean?

GREGERS: You have dived down and tangled yourself in seaweed.

HJALMAR: Are you referring to that near fatal shot that broke my father's wing—and mine too?

GREGERS: Not exactly. I'm not saying that your wing has been broken. But you've wandered into a poisonous marsh, Hjalmar. You have contracted an insidious disease, and plunged down to die in the dark.

HJALMAR: I? Die in the dark? Come on, Gregers, you really have to stop talking such nonsense.

GREGERS: Don't be afraid. I'll find a way to bring you to the surface again. I too have a purpose in life now. I discovered it yesterday.

HJALMAR: That may be; but please leave me out of it. You can be sure that—apart from my natural melancholy, of course—I am as happy as any man could be.

GREGERS: That is a result of the marsh poison.

HJALMAR: Please, Gregers, stop going on about diseases and poisons. I'm not used to that kind of talk. In my house, nobody ever speaks to me about unpleasant things.

GREGERS: That I can well believe.

HJALMAR: It's not good for me, you see. And around

here there are no marsh poisons, as you put it. The poor photographer's home is humble, I know—and my circumstances are limited. But I am an inventor, and I am the family breadwinner. That helps me rise above my mean surroundings. —Ah, here comes lunch!

(Gina and Hedvig bring bottles of ale, a decanter of brandy, glasses, etc. At the same time, Relling and Molvik enter from the passage; they are both witnout hat or overcoat. Molvik is dressed in black.)

GINA: *(placing the things upon the table)* Ah, you've come just in time.

RELLING: Once Molvik smelled herring salad, there was no holding him back. —Good morning again, Ekdal.

HJALMAR: Gregers, let me introduce you to Mr. Molvik. And this is Doctor—oh, but you know Relling already, don't you?

GREGERS: Slightly.

RELLING: Oh, Mr. Werle, junior! Yes, we've had a few little skirmishes up at the Hoidal mill. You've just moved in?

GREGERS: I moved in this morning.

RELLING: Molvik and I live right below you; so you don't have to go far for a doctor and a clergyman, if you ever need anything in that line.

GREGERS: Thanks, it's not impossible. Yesterday there were thirteen of us at the table.

HJALMAR: Oh, let's not bring up unpleasant subjects again!

RELLING: Relax, Ekdal. I truly doubt that the finger of fate is pointing at you.

HJALMAR: I hope not, for my family's sake. But let's sit down now. Let's eat, drink, and be merry.

GREGERS: Shouldn't we wait for your father?

HJALMAR: No, his meal will be delivered to him later. Let's go!

(The men seat themselves at table, and eat and drink. Gina and Hedvig go in and out and wait on them.)

RELLING: Molvik was really plastered yesterday, Mrs. Ekdal.

GINA: Really? Again?

RELLING: Didn't you hear him when I brought him home last night?

GINA: No, I can't say I did.

RELLING: That's just as well, because Molvik was disgusting last night.

GINA: Is that true, Molvik?

MOLVIK: Let us draw a veil over last night's proceedings. That sort of behavior bears no relation to my true self.

RELLING: *(to Gregers)* It comes over him like a sort of possession, and then I have to go out on the town with him. You see, Mr. Molvik is demonic.

GREGERS: Demonic?

RELLING: Molvik is demonic, yes.

GREGERS: Hm.

RELLING: And demonic natures are not meant to walk a straight line in this world. They have to stagger a bit now and then. —So are you still sticking it out at that disgusting old lumber mill?

GREGERS: I have been sticking it out there until now.

84

RELLING: And did you ever manage to settle that claim you were always talking about?

GREGERS: Claim? *(understands him)* Oh, I see.

HJALMAR: What claim is that, Gregers?

GREGERS: He's talking nonsense.

RELLING: I'm not kidding! He used to go around to all the workmen's cabins with what he called "the claim of the ideal."

GREGERS: I was young then.

RELLING: You're right. You were very young. And as for the claim of the ideal, you never got it settled while I was up there.

GREGERS: Or since either.

RELLING: Ah, so you've learned to lower the price, I guess.

GREGERS: Never, when I'm dealing with an authentic human being.

HJALMAR: That sounds reasonable. Bring the butter, Gina.

RELLING: And a slice of bacon for Molvik.

MOLVIK: Ugh. No bacon! *(a knock at the storeroom door)*

HJALMAR: Open the trapdoor, Hedvig; grandfather wants to come out. *(Hedvig goes over and opens the door a little way; Ekdal enters with a fresh rabbit skin. She closes the door after him.)*

EKDAL: Good morning, gentlemen! Good hunting today. Shot a big one.

HJALMAR: And you went ahead and skinned it without waiting for me!

EKDAL: Salted it too. It's nice tender meat, rabbit

meat. And it's sweet; tastes like sugar. Enjoy your lunch, gentlemen! *(goes into his room)*

MOLVIK: *(rising)* Excuse me—I can't—got to get downstairs before I—

RELLING: Drink some seltzer, man!

MOLVIK: *(hurrying away)* Ugh—ugh! *(goes out by the passage door)*

RELLING: *(to Hjalmar)* Let us drain a glass to the old hunter.

HJALMAR: *(clinks glasses with him)* To the old sportsman looking death in the face!

RELLING: To the grey-haired— *(drinks)* By the way, is his hair grey or white?

HJALMAR: Something in between. As a matter of fact, he doesn't have many hairs left of any color.

RELLING: Well, well, you can get through life with a wig. You know, you're a happy man, Ekdal. You have an important purpose in life—

HJALMAR: And I do work, I can tell you.

RELLING: And you've got your wonderful wife, shuffling quietly in and out in her felt slippers, with that little waddle of hers, making your life cozy and easy—

HJALMAR: Yes, Gina— *(nods to her)* —you are a wonderful companion on the path of life.

GINA: Oh, don't sit there making fun of me.

RELLING: And then you have your Hedvig too, Ekdal!

HJALMAR: *(affected)* My child, yes! My child comes before everything! Come here, Hedvig, come to me. *(strokes her hair)* What day is it tomorrow, eh?

HEDVIG: *(shaking him)* Oh no, you have to keep quiet about that, daddy.

HJALMAR: I am cut to the heart when I think what a poor occasion it will be. Just a little party in the storeroom—

HEDVIG: Oh, but that's just how I like it!

RELLING: Just wait until that wonderful invention is finished, Hedvig!

HJALMAR: Yes indeed—then you'll see—! Hedvig, I have decided to secure your future. You're going to live in comfort for the rest of your life. That will be the poor inventor's only reward.

HEDVIG: *(whispering, with her arms around his neck)* My dear, sweet daddy!

RELLING: *(to Gregers)* Isn't it nice for a change to sit in the middle of a happy family at a table full of good food?

HJALMAR: Yes, I really love these hours at the table.

GREGERS: If you want my opinion, I don't breathe marsh gas very well.

RELLING: Marsh gas?

HJALMAR: Oh, don't start that stuff again!

GINA: The Lord knows there is no gas in this house, Mr. Werle. I give the place a good airing every day.

GREGERS: *(leaves the table)* The poisonous vapors I'm talking about can't be just aired out.

HJALMAR: Poisonous vapors!

GINA: What do you say to that, Hjalmar!

RELLING: I beg your pardon—but isn't it possible you brought noxious poisons from the mines with you?

GREGERS: It's just like you to say that what I bring into this house is poisoned.

RELLING: *(goes up to him)* Listen, Mr. Werle, junior. I have a strong suspicion that you're still carrying that "claim of the ideal" in your coat pocket. The uncut version.

GREGERS: I carry it in my heart.

RELLING: Well, wherever you carry it, you'd better not stake your claim here, as long as I'm on the premises.

GREGERS: And if I do in spite of you?

RELLING: Then you'll get thrown down the stairs head first. Take it as a warning.

HJALMAR: *(rising)* Come now, Relling—!

GREGERS: Yes, yes, please throw me out—

GINA: *(interposing between them)* We won't have any of that. But I must say, Mr. Werle, you have little right to talk about poisons and vapors after the mess you made with your stove.

(A knock at the passage door.)

HEDVIG: Someone's knocking, mother.

HJALMAR: We're getting flooded with people!

GINA: I'll go see. *(goes over and opens the door, starts, and draws back)* Oh—oh, dear! *(Werle, in a fur coat, advances one step into the room)*

WERLE: Excuse me. I think my son is staying here.

GINA: *(with a gulp)* Yes.

HJALMAR: *(approaching him)* Mr. Werle, won't you join us for—?

WERLE: Thank you, I only want to speak to my son.

GREGERS: What do you want? Here I am.

WERLE: I want a few words with you, in your room.

GREGERS: In my room? Very well— *(about to go)*

GINA: No, no, your room's not in a fit state—

WERLE: Well then, downstairs in the hallway. I need a few words with you alone.

HJALMAR: You can have your talk here, sir. Come into the other room, Relling. *(Hjalmar and Relling go off to the right. Gina takes Hedvig with her into the kitchen.)*

GREGERS: *(after a short pause)* Well, here we are, alone.

WERLE: From something you said last night, and from your coming here to the Ekdals, I have an idea that you're planning something unpleasant for me.

GREGERS: I am planning to open Hjalmar Ekdal's eyes. He will see his position as it really is, that's all.

WERLE: Is that the purpose in life you spoke about yesterday?

GREGERS: Yes. You've left me no other.

WERLE: Then I'm the one who's poisoned your mind, Gregers?

GREGERS: You have poisoned my whole life. I'm not thinking about mother and all that— But it's thanks to you that I am continually tortured by a guilty conscience.

WERLE: Ah! So it's your conscience that's bothering you, is it?

GREGERS: I ought to have stood up to you when the

trap was being laid for Lieutenant Ekdal. I should have warned him. I had a suspicion about what was in store for him.

WERLE: Yes, that's when you should have spoken up.

GREGERS: I didn't have the courage. I was so cowardly and passive. I was totally afraid of you—not just then, but long after.

WERLE: It seems you're over that fear now, at least.

GREGERS: Yes, fortunately. The wrong done to old Ekdal, both by me and by—others, can never be undone. But I can liberate Hjalmar from the falsehood and deception that are ruining his life.

WERLE: And you think that will be a kindness?

GREGERS: I haven't the slightest doubt.

WERLE: You think our noble photographer is the sort of man to appreciate such friendly services?

GREGERS: Yes, I do.

WERLE: Hm. We'll see.

GREGERS: If I'm to go on living, I must find some cure for my sickly conscience.

WERLE: There is no cure. Your conscience has been sickly from birth. It's a legacy from your mother, Gregers—the only one she left you.

GREGERS: *(with a scornful half-smile)* You still haven't forgiven her for not bringing you the fortune you expected?

WERLE: Let's stick to the point. Is this your purpose, then, to lead Hjalmar Ekdal back into what you consider to be the right direction?

GREGERS: Yes, that is my firm intention.

WERLE: Well, in that case I might have spared myself the trouble of this visit. I suppose there's no use in my asking you to come home with me?

GREGERS: No.

WERLE: And you won't come into the firm either?

GREGERS: No.

WERLE: All right. But since I'm thinking of remarrying, your share in the estate will come to you at once.

GREGERS: *(quickly)* No, I don't want that.

WERLE: You don't want it?

GREGERS: No, I couldn't take it. My conscience wouldn't allow it.

WERLE: *(after a pause)* Are you going up to the mill again?

GREGERS: No. I'm no longer your employee.

WERLE: So what are you going to do?

GREGERS: Fulfill my purpose in life, nothing more.

WERLE: Yes, but afterward? What will you live on?

GREGERS: I've saved a little salary.

WERLE: How long will that last?

GREGERS: I think it will last out my time.

WERLE: What does that mean?

GREGERS: I refuse to answer any more questions.

WERLE: Goodbye then, Gregers.

GREGERS: Goodbye.

(Werle goes.)

HJALMAR: *(peeping in)* Is he gone?

GREGERS: Yes.

(Hjalmar and Relling enter; also Gina and Hedvig from the kitchen.)

RELLING: The lunch was a disaster.

GREGERS: Put on your coat, Hjalmar. I want you to take a long walk with me.

HJALMAR: Gladly. What did your father want? Anything to do with me?

GREGERS: Come along. We must have our talk. I'll go get my overcoat. *(goes out by the passage door)*

GINA: Don't go with him, Ekdal.

RELLING: No, don't. Stay where you are.

HJALMAR: *(gets his hat and overcoat)* Nonsense! When an old friend feels compelled to open himself to me in private—

RELLING: The devil take him—don't you see the fellow's mad, cracked, demented!

GINA: See what I told you? His mother had crazy fits like that from time to time.

HJALMAR: Then he has all the more need of a helpful friend. *(to Gina)* Be sure that dinner is ready on time. Goodbye for now. *(goes out by the passage door)*

RELLING: It's a great pity the fellow didn't go straight to hell through one of the Hoidal mines.

GINA: Good Lord! What makes you say that?

RELLING: *(muttering)* Oh, I have my own reasons.

GINA: Do you really think he's crazy?

RELLING: No, unfortunately, no crazier than most people. But there's one disease he's got in his system.

GINA: What's that?

RELLING: I'll tell you, Mrs. Ekdal. He's suffering from an acute attack of integrity.

GINA: Integrity?

HEDVIG: Is that a kind of disease?

RELLING: It's a national disease; but it only appears sporadically. *(nods to Gina)* Thanks for the lunch. *(he goes out by the passage door)*

GINA: *(moving restlessly to and fro)* Ugh, that Gregers Werle—he always was a disgusting creature.

HEDVIG: *(standing by the table and looking searchingly at her)* All this seems to me very peculiar.

ACT 4

Hjalmar Ekdal's studio. A photograph has just been taken; a camera with the cloth over it, a pedestal, two chairs, a folding table, etc., are standing out in the room. Afternoon light; the sun is going down. A little later it begins to grow dark.

Gina stands in the passage doorway, with a little box and a wet glass plate in her hand, and is speaking to somebody outside.

GINA: Yes, of course I will. When I promise something, I do it. I'll have the first dozen ready on Monday. Good afternoon.

(Noise of someone going downstairs. Gina shuts the door, slips the plate into the box, and puts it into the covered camera.)

HEDVIG: *(comes in from the kitchen)* They've gone?

GINA: *(tidying up)* Yes, thank heaven, I finally got rid of them.

HEDVIG: Do you know why daddy hasn't come home yet?

GINA: Maybe he's down in Relling's room?

HEDVIG: No, he's not. I just ran down the kitchen stairs to see.

GINA: And his dinner's getting cold.

HEDVIG: Why is daddy late? He never misses dinner!

94

GINA: Oh, he'll be here soon enough. You'll see.

HEDVIG: I wish he'd come. Everything seems so peculiar today.

GINA: *(calls out)* He's here! *(Hjalmar Ekdal comes in at the passage door)*

HEDVIG: *(going to him)* Daddy! We've been waiting and waiting for you!

GINA: *(glancing sidelong at him)* You've been gone a long time, Ekdal.

HJALMAR: *(without looking at her)* I was gone a long time, yes. *(He takes off his overcoat. Gina and Hedvig go to help him, but he motions them away.)*

GINA: Have you had dinner with Werle?

HJALMAR: *(hanging up his coat)* No.

GINA: *(going toward the kitchen door)* Then I'll bring you some.

HJALMAR: Forget about dinner. I want nothing to eat.

HEDVIG: *(going nearer to him)* Don't you feel well, daddy?

HJALMAR: Feel well? Oh yes, I feel well enough. We've had an exhausting walk, Gregers and I.

GINA: Why did you walk so much, Ekdal? You're not used to it.

HJALMAR: Ah, a man has to get used to a lot of things in this world. *(wanders about the room)* Was anyone here while I was out?

GINA: Just that couple.

HJALMAR: Any new orders?

GINA: No, not today.

95

HEDVIG: We'll get some tomorrow, daddy, you'll see.

HJALMAR: Let us hope. Tomorrow I intend to start to work hard.

HEDVIG: Tomorrow! Did you forget what day it is tomorrow?

HJALMAR: Yes, that's right. Well, the day after tomorrow, then. From now on, I intend to do everything myself. I don't want anyone helping me.

GINA: What's the sense of that, Hjalmar? You'll only make yourself miserable. I can take care of the photography all right, and you can keep working on your invention.

HEDVIG: And what about the wild duck, daddy—and all those hens and rabbits!

HJALMAR: Don't talk about that nonsense! Starting tomorrow, I'll never set foot in the storeroom again.

HEDVIG: Oh, but daddy, you promised we would have a little party tomorrow.

HJALMAR: Hm, that's true. Well, from the day after tomorrow, then. I'd really like to wring the neck of that damned wild duck!

HEDVIG: *(shrieks)* The wild duck!

GINA: What a thing to say!

HEDVIG: *(pulling his arm)* But daddy, it's my wild duck!

HJALMAR: That's the only reason I don't do it. I haven't the heart—I can't bring myself to—because of you, Hedvig. But in my inner being I feel I should. I won't tolerate a single creature under my roof that's associated with that man.

GINA: Why, good heavens, even if grandfather did get it from that Peterson—

HJALMAR: *(wandering about)* There are certain claims—what shall I call them? There are certain claims of the ideal—certain obligations, that a man can't ignore without destroying his soul.

HEDVIG: *(going after him)* But think of the wild duck, the poor wild duck!

HJALMAR: *(stops)* I told you I would spare it—for your sake. I won't touch a hair of its—I mean, I'll spare it. I have bigger problems than that to deal with. But why don't you go out for a little while, Hedvig, as usual. It's dark enough for you now.

HEDVIG: No, I don't want to go out now.

HJALMAR: Yes, go out. You seem to be blinking a lot. All these gases in here are unhealthy for you. The air is very thick under this roof.

HEDVIG: All right, I'll run down the kitchen stairs and go for a walk. Daddy, please don't hurt the wild duck while I'm gone.

HJALMAR: Not a feather on its head shall be touched. *(draws her to him)* You and I, Hedvig—we two! Well, run along.

(Hedvig nods to her parents and goes out through the kitchen.)

HJALMAR: *(walks about without looking up)* Gina.

GINA: Yes?

HJALMAR: From tomorrow on—well, let's say from the day after tomorrow on—I will keep the household accounts myself.

GINA: Now you want to keep the accounts too?

HJALMAR: Yes, or at least check the receipts.

GINA: My Lord! That's easy enough.

HJALMAR: I'm not so sure. You certainly seem to make the money go a long way. *(stops and looks at her)* How do you manage it?

GINA: Me and Hedvig don't need much.

HJALMAR: Is it true my father is paid very well for the copying he does for Mr. Werle?

GINA: I don't know if he gets paid anything special. I don't know what they pay for that sort of work.

HJALMAR: Well, how much does he make, roughly speaking? Tell me!

GINA: It varies. Roughly speaking, it's about what he costs us, with a little pocket money left over.

HJALMAR: About what he costs us! And you never told me this before!

GINA: No, how could I? You were so happy to think he got everything from you.

HJALMAR: But he actually gets it from Mr. Werle.

GINA: He can spare it.

HJALMAR: Light the lamp for me, please!

GINA: *(lighting the lamp)* We don't know if it's Mr. Werle himself. It could be Graberg—

HJALMAR: Don't be evasive.

GINA: I don't know anything about it. I only thought—

HJALMAR: Hm!

GINA: I didn't get that copying job for grandfather. Berta did, when she used to come to see us.

HJALMAR: It seems to me your voice is different.

GINA: *(putting the lampshade on)* It is?

HJALMAR: And your hands are shaking, aren't they?

GINA: *(firmly)* Spit it out, Ekdal. What has he been saying about me?

HJALMAR: Is it true—can it possibly be true—that there was something between you and Mr. Werle when you were working there?

GINA: It's not true. Not then. Mr. Werle was always after me, that's true enough. And his wife thought that something was going on. And she made a big fuss about it. She beat me and pulled me by the hair— Yes! She did that . . . until finally I quit my job.

HJALMAR: What about afterward?

GINA: Afterward I went back home. And my mother— well, she wasn't the woman you thought she was, Ekdal. She kept badgering me about one thing and another because Mr. Werle had become a widower by that time.

HJALMAR: Well, what then?

GINA: I suppose you have to know. He wouldn't leave me alone until he got his way.

HJALMAR: *(striking his hands together)* And this is the mother of my child! How could you hide this from me?

GINA: That was wrong, I know. I should have told you long ago.

HJALMAR: You should have told me immediately. I would have known what kind of woman you were.

GINA: Would you have married me anyway?

HJALMAR: Of course not!

GINA: That's just why I didn't tell you then. I'd gotten to love you so much, you see. And I couldn't make myself so utterly miserable—

HJALMAR: *(walks about)* And this is the mother of my Hedvig! And to think I owe everything— *(kicks at a chair)* everything I call home—to a favored predecessor! Oh, that goddamn Werle!

GINA: Are you sorry about the fourteen—the fifteen years we lived together?

HJALMAR: *(standing in front of her)* Aren't you sorry about every day, every hour—aren't you sorry about the web of deceit you've spun around me? Answer me that! Don't you spend all your time in regret and remorse?

GINA: My dear Ekdal. I spend all my time looking after the house and all the work I have to do—

HJALMAR: You never think about your past?

GINA: No. God knows I've almost forgotten all those old things.

HJALMAR: Oh, your callow, unfeeling contentment! I find it revolting. Think about it—you're not sorry a bit!

GINA: Tell me this, Ekdal—what would have become of you without a wife like me?

HJALMAR: A wife like you!

GINA: Yes. I've always been more practical and businesslike. Of course I'm a year or two older.

HJALMAR: What would have become of me!

GINA: You had taken a few wrong turns when you first met me, you can't deny that.

HJALMAR: Wrong turns you call it? You have no understanding of what a man feels when he's overcome with grief and despair—especially a man of my passionate nature.

GINA: Well, well, that may be true. And I shouldn't criticize you either because you became a real good husband as soon as you had a home of your own. And here we got everything so nice and cozy; and me and Hedvig was just beginning to think we could spend a little on ourselves in the way of food and clothes.

HJALMAR: Yes, in a swamp of deceit.

GINA: I wish to hell that miserable creature had never set foot in our house!

HJALMAR: I also used to think we had a happy home. It was a delusion. Where will I find the inspiration now to complete my invention? Maybe it will die with me. And it will be your past, Gina, that killed it.

GINA: *(nearly crying)* Don't say such things, Ekdal. I only wanted what was best for you!

HJALMAR: What becomes of the breadwinner's dream now? When I lay there on the couch, thinking of my invention, I had a presentment that it would use up all my energy. I felt that the day I held the patent in my hand—that day—would bring my—release. And it was my fantasy that you would live on after me as the prosperous widow of the dead inventor.

GINA: *(drying her tears)* Oh don't talk like that, Ekdal. I pray God I never see the day I'm a widow!

HJALMAR: Well, the dream is over. It's vanished now. Vanished!

(Gregers Werle opens the passage door cautiously and looks in.)

GREGERS: *(comes forward, his face beaming with satisfaction, and holds out both his hands to them)* My dear friends—! *(looks from one to the other, and whispers to Hjalmar)* Haven't you done it yet?

HJALMAR: *(aloud)* It's done.

GREGERS: It is?

HJALMAR: I have experienced the bitterest moments of my life.

GREGERS: But also the most exalting.

HJALMAR: Well, at any rate, we got through it for now.

GINA: May God forgive you, Mr. Werle.

GREGERS: *(in great surprise)* I don't understand this.

HJALMAR: What don't you understand?

GREGERS: After such a great crisis—a crisis that should result in a completely new life—a new life—a relationship founded on truth, and free of deceit—

HJALMAR: Yes, I know, I know.

GREGERS: I thoroughly expected, when I entered this room, to see a husband and wife transfigured and radiant. And what I see instead is nothing but dejection, oppression, gloom—

GINA: How's this? *(takes off the lampshade)*

GREGERS: You refuse to understand me, Mrs. Ekdal. I suppose you need time. But you, Hjalmar? You must feel blessed by this wonderful illumination.

HJALMAR: Of course I do. Yes, I do—sort of.

GREGERS: Because there's nothing in the world that

can compare with the joy of forgiveness, of redeeming the guilt of a sinner with love.

HJALMAR: You think it's so easy for a man to drink the bitter cup I've just drained?

GREGERS: No, not an ordinary man, perhaps. But a man like you—!

HJALMAR: Good God! I know that all right. But don't rush me, Gregers. It takes a little time, you know.

GREGERS: You have a lot of the wild duck in you, Hjalmar.

(*Relling has come in at the passage door.*)

RELLING: Hello! Are we still going on about the wild duck?

HJALMAR: Yes, Mr. Werle's wing-wounded trophy of the hunt.

RELLING: Mr. Werle—? So you're talking about him?

HJALMAR: Him—and all of us.

RELLING: (*in an undertone to Gregers*) I hope the devil kicks you in the ass!

HJALMAR: What are you saying?

RELLING: Only expressing a wish that this quack would get the hell out of here. If he stays, he's perfectly capable of destroying you both.

GREGERS: These two will not be destroyed, Mr. Relling. I won't speak for Hjalmar—we know him already. As for his wife, I'm sure she has trust and sincerity deep down inside her—

GINA: (*almost crying*) Then you should have let me be.

RELLING: *(to Gregers)* Is it too much to ask you exactly what you want from this house?

GREGERS: I want to lay the foundations of a true marriage.

RELLING: You don't think Ekdal's marriage is good enough as it is?

GREGERS: It's as good a marriage as many others, unfortunately. But it has never been a true marriage.

HJALMAR: You have never appreciated the claims of the ideal, Relling.

RELLING: Bullshit, my friend! Excuse me, Mr. Werle, how many true marriages have you seen in your life? In round numbers.

GREGERS: Probably not one.

RELLING: I haven't either.

GREGERS: But I've seen hundreds of the other kind. And I've had the opportunity to witness up close how such a marriage can ruin both partners.

HJALMAR: It can sap a man's whole moral character, that's what's so terrible.

RELLING: Well, I've never actually been married, so I won't pretend to speak with authority. But I do know this, that a child is involved in the marriage too. And a child should be left in peace.

HJALMAR: Oh—Hedvig! my poor Hedvig!

RELLING: Yes, please have the grace to keep Hedvig out of all this. You two are grown-ups. You're free to mess up your lives as much as you want. But be careful with Hedvig, I tell you, or you may do her a great injury.

HJALMAR: An injury!

RELLING: Or she may do herself an injury—and others too, perhaps.

GINA: How could you know that, Relling?

HJALMAR: There's no immediate danger to her eyes, is there?

RELLING: I'm not talking about her eyes. Hedvig is at a critical age. She may get all kinds of ideas into her head.

GINA: You're right. She's doing it already! She's taken to poking at the fire, out in the kitchen. She calls it playing at burning up. I'm often scared she'll really set fire to the house.

RELLING: There, you see? I knew it.

GREGERS: *(to Relling)* How do you explain it?

RELLING: *(sullenly)* Her body's changing, sir.

HJALMAR: As long as the child has me! As long as I'm still alive—! *(a knock at the door)*

GINA: Quiet, Ekdal, there's someone at the door. *(calls out)* Come in!

(Mrs. Soerby, in outdoor clothes, comes in.)

MRS. SOERBY: Good evening.

GINA: *(going toward her)* Berta—it's you!

MRS. SOERBY: Of course it's me. Am I here at the wrong time?

HJALMAR: No, not at all. A messenger from that house—

MRS. SOERBY: *(to Gina)* To tell you the truth, I was hoping the men of the house wouldn't be here

105

now. I just came to have a little chat with you, and to say goodbye.

GINA: Oh, you're going away?

MRS. SOERBY: Tomorrow morning—up to Hoidal. Mr. Werle left this afternoon. *(lightly to Gregers)* He asked to be remembered to you.

GINA: Ah, really!

HJALMAR: So Mr. Werle is off? And now you're joining him?

MRS. SOERBY: Yes, what do you say to that, Ekdal?

HJALMAR: I say: watch out!

GREGERS: I can explain. My father and Mrs. Soerby are going to get married.

HJALMAR: Married! To her?

GINA: Oh, Berta! Has it finally happened?

RELLING: *(his voice quivering a little)* Is this really true?

MRS. SOERBY: Yes, my dear Relling, it's true.

RELLING: You're going to marry again?

MRS. SOERBY: That's what it looks like. Werle got a special license, and we're going to be married very quietly, up at the mill.

GREGERS: Then I suppose I should wish you happiness, like a good stepson.

MRS. SOERBY: Thank you very much—if you're sincere. I certainly hope it *will* mean happiness, both for Werle and for me.

RELLING: You have every reason to expect it. Mr. Werle never gets drunk, as far as I know; and I can't imagine he's in the wife-beating business, like the late lamented horse doctor.

MRS. SOERBY: All right, let Soerby rest in peace. He had his assets too.

RELLING: Mr. Werle has richer assets, I believe.

MRS. SOERBY: At any rate, he hasn't wasted everything that was best in him. Anyone who does that must take the consequences.

RELLING: Tonight I go out with Molvik.

MRS. SOERBY: Don't, Relling. For my sake.

RELLING: What else can I do? *(to Hjalmar)* If you'd like to come along, you're welcome.

GINA: No, thank you. Hjalmar doesn't go in for that sort of thing.

HJALMAR: *(half aloud, in vexation)* Oh, please shut up!

RELLING: Goodbye, Mrs.—Werle. *(goes out through the passage door)*

GREGERS: *(to Mrs. Soerby)* You and Dr. Relling seem on pretty intimate terms.

MRS. SOERBY: Yes, we've known each other a long time. Once it seemed that things might have developed between us.

GREGERS: Lucky for you they didn't.

MRS. SOERBY: You can certainly say that. But I've always been hesitant about acting on impulse. A woman can't afford to throw herself away.

GREGERS: Does it worry you at all that I might tell my father about this old relationship?

MRS. SOERBY: Naturally I told him all about it myself.

GREGERS: You did?

MRS. SOERBY: Your father knows everything there is to know about me that contains a grain of truth.

I told him absolutely everything as soon as I guessed at his intentions.

GREGERS: That makes you more honest than most people.

MRS. SOERBY: I have always been honest. It's the best policy for a woman.

HJALMAR: What do you say to that, Gina?

GINA: Women aren't all alike. Some are made one way, some another.

MRS. SOERBY: Well, Gina, I believe the wisest thing is to do it my way. And Werle hasn't hidden anything either. That's the basis for the great bond between us. He can talk to me now as openly as a child. That's what he never had a chance to do before. Imagine a healthy and vigorous man passing the best years of his life listening to sermons on his sins! And often those sermons were about the most imaginary offenses—or so it seems to me.

GINA: I'm sure that's true.

GREGERS: If the ladies are going to harp on this theme, I'd better leave.

MRS. SOERBY: You can stay as far as I'm concerned. I won't say one more word. But I wanted you to know I'd done nothing secret or underhand. You probably think I've come into a great piece of luck; and I suppose I have, in a way. But I don't think I'm getting any more than I'm giving. Anyway, I'll always stand by him. And I'm able to care for him like no one else, now that he's getting helpless.

HJALMAR: Helpless?

GREGERS: *(to Mrs. Soerby)* Ssh, don't talk about that here.

MRS. SOERBY: There's no sense hiding it any longer, however he'd like to. He's going blind.

HJALMAR: *(starts)* He's going blind?

GINA: Lots of people do.

MRS. SOERBY: You can imagine what that means to a businessman. Well, I'm going to try my best to make my eyes take the place of his. But I have to go. There's so much to do. Oh, by the way, Ekdal, I was asked to tell you that if there's anything Werle can do for you, you should just ask Graberg.

GREGERS: That is an offer I am certain Hjalmar Ekdal will decline.

MRS. SOERBY: Really? I don't believe he was always so—

GINA: He's right, Berta, Hjalmar doesn't need anything from Mr. Werle now.

HJALMAR: *(slowly, and with emphasis)* Please give my regards to your future husband, and tell him I intend very soon to call upon Mr. Graberg—

GREGERS: You don't mean that!

HJALMAR: To call upon Mr. Graberg, I say, and ask for an accounting of what I owe his employer. I will pay that debt of honor—ha! ha! ha!—that's a good name for it! Anyway, I will pay the whole sum with five percent interest.

GINA: But, Ekdal dear, we don't have that kind of money.

HJALMAR: Be so good as to inform your future husband that I am working very hard at my invention. Please tell him that what sustains me in this exhausting task is the desire to free myself from a painful burden of debt. That is my reason for proceeding with the invention. All the profits will be devoted to releasing me from my pecuniary obligations to your future husband.

MRS. SOERBY: Something has happened here.

HJALMAR: You are right.

MRS. SOERBY: Well, goodbye. I had something else I wanted to talk to you about, Gina. But it will have to wait for another time. Goodbye.

(Hjalmar and Gregers bow silently. Gina follows Mrs. Soerby to the door.)

HJALMAR: Don't go beyond that door, Gina!

(Mrs. Soerby goes; Gina shuts the door after her.)

HJALMAR: There now, Gregers, that debt is paid.

GREGERS: It will soon be paid, anyway.

HJALMAR: I think you can say I conducted myself correctly.

GREGERS: You are the man I always thought you were.

HJALMAR: There are times when it is impossible to ignore the claim of the ideal. Yet, as the head of a family, I cannot but groan and wriggle under this burden. It is no easy thing for a man without capital to try to repay a long-standing obligation, over which the dust of oblivion has, so to speak, collected. But there's no other way: my humanity demands it.

GREGERS: *(laying his hand on Hjalmar's shoulder)* Dear Hjalmar—wasn't it good I came?

HJALMAR: Yes.

GREGERS: Isn't it good to know the truth of your situation?

HJALMAR: *(somewhat impatiently)* Yes, of course. But there's one thing that violates my sense of justice.

GREGERS: What's that?

HJALMAR: Well, it's just that—but I don't know if I should talk like this about your father.

GREGERS: Say whatever you please.

HJALMAR: Well, don't you find it revolting to think that he, not I, is the one to have created the true marriage?

GREGERS: How can you say such a thing?

HJALMAR: Because it's quite obvious. The marriage between your father and Mrs. Soerby will be based on complete confidence, on absolute honesty from both sides. They are hiding nothing from each other. They keep no hidden secrets. They have a relationship of mutual forgiveness.

GREGERS: Well, what if they do?

HJALMAR: Well, isn't that it exactly? Didn't you say yourself that this was just the way to lay the foundations of a true marriage?

GREGERS: But that's an entirely different thing, Hjalmar. You're not going to compare yourself or your wife with those two—. Well, you know what I mean.

HJALMAR: Say what you will, there is something here that offends my sense of justice. It really looks as if there were no God ruling the world.

GINA: Ekdal, don't say such things.

GREGERS: Hm. We'd better not get into that.

HJALMAR: And yet, I sense a guiding hand of fate in all this. He *is* going blind.

GINA: Oh, you can't be sure of that.

HJALMAR: There's no doubt about it. We shouldn't doubt it, anyway, because it's a form of righteous retribution. He has in his time blinded a trusting, faithful partner—

GREGERS: He's blinded many.

HJALMAR: And now comes this inexorable, mysterious power to demand Werle's own eyes.

GINA: You have no right to say such dreadful things! You're scaring me.

HJALMAR: It is good, now and then, to plunge deep into the dark side of life.

(Hedvig, in her hat and cloak, comes in by the passage door. She is pleasurably excited and out of breath.)

GINA: Are you back already?

HEDVIG: Yes, I didn't want to stay out anymore. It was a good thing too, because I just met someone at the door.

HJALMAR: Mrs. Soerby?

HEDVIG: Yes.

HJALMAR: *(walks up and down)* I trust you have seen her for the last time.

(Silence. Hedvig, disheartened, looks first at one and then the other, trying to make out their attitudes.)

HEDVIG: *(approaching, coaxingly)* Daddy.

HJALMAR: Well, what do you want, Hedvig?

HEDVIG: Mrs. Soerby brought something with her for me.

HJALMAR: *(stops)* For you?

HEDVIG: Yes. A present for tomorrow.

GINA: Berta always gives you something on your birthday.

HJALMAR: What is it?

HEDVIG: Oh, it's a secret now. Mother is supposed to give it to me when I wake up tomorrow.

HJALMAR: What's the mystery? Am I supposed to be kept in the dark?

HEDVIG: *(quickly)* Oh no, you can see it if you want. It's a long letter. *(takes the letter out of her cloak pocket)*

HJALMAR: She gave you a letter too?

HEDVIG: Only a letter. The rest comes later, I suppose. But just think—a letter! I never had a letter before. And look, it says "Miss" on the envelope. *(reads)* "Miss Hedvig Ekdal." Just think—that's me!

HJALMAR: Let me see that letter.

HEDVIG: *(hands it to him)* Here.

HJALMAR: It's in Mr. Werle's handwriting.

GINA: Are you sure, Hjalmar?

HJALMAR: See for yourself.

GINA: Oh, what do I know about such things?

HJALMAR: Hedvig, may I open the letter—and read it?

HEDVIG: Yes, of course, if you want to.

GINA: Not tonight, Hjalmar. It's supposed to be for tomorrow.

HEDVIG: *(softly)* Oh, let him read it! I'm sure it's something nice. And that will make daddy happy. And everything will be all right again.

HJALMAR: I can open it then?

HEDVIG: Please do, daddy. I can't wait to know what it says.

HJALMAR: All right. *(opens the letter, takes out a paper, reads it through with evident amazement)* What is this—!

GINA: What does it say?

HEDVIG: Yes, daddy, tell us!

HJALMAR: Be quiet. *(reads it through again; he has turned pale, but says with self-control)* It's a deed of gift, Hedvig.

HEDVIG: It is? What do I get?

HJALMAR: Read it for yourself.

(Hedvig goes over and reads for a time by the lamp.)

HJALMAR: *(half aloud, clenching his hands)* First the eyes! The eyes. And now this letter!

HEDVIG: *(stops reading)* Yes, but this seems to be for grandfather.

HJALMAR: *(takes the letter from her)* Do you understand this, Gina?

GINA: I don't know anything about it. Tell me what it is.

HJALMAR: Mr. Werle writes to Hedvig that her old grandfather won't have to bother with copying any more. From now on, he can draw a hundred crowns a month from the office.

GREGERS: Aha!

HEDVIG: A hundred crowns, mother! That's what it says.

GINA: How lovely for grandfather!

HJALMAR: —a hundred crowns a month as long as he needs it—that means, of course, as long as he lives.

GINA: Well, he's provided for, poor dear.

HJALMAR: But there's more here that you didn't read, Hedvig. Afterward, the gift is transferred to you.

HEDVIG: To me! All that money?

HJALMAR: You get the same amount your whole life. Do you hear that, Gina?

GINA: Yes, I hear.

HEDVIG: Just think—all that money for me! *(shakes him)* Daddy, daddy, doesn't this make you happy?

HJALMAR: *(eluding her)* Happy! *(walks about)* What a future—what a perspective—this opens up to my eyes! It's Hedvig, Hedvig, who inherits all this largesse!

GINA: Yes, because it's Hedvig's birthday—

HEDVIG: And it'll belong to you, daddy! You know I'll give all the money to you and mother.

HJALMAR: To your mother, yes! And that's just the point.

GREGERS: Hjalmar, he's laying a trap for you.

HJALMAR: You think it's another trap?

GREGERS: When he came here this morning, he said: Hjalmar Ekdal is not the man you think he is.

HJALMAR: Not the man—!

GREGERS: You'll see, he said.

HJALMAR: He meant I could be bribed!

HEDVIG: Mother, what is this all about?

GINA: Go take off your things.

(Hedvig goes out by the kitchen door, half crying.)

GREGERS: Yes, Hjalmar. The time has come for you to prove who was right, him or me.

HJALMAR: *(slowly tears the paper across, lays both pieces on the table, and says)* This is my answer.

GREGERS: That is what I expected.

HJALMAR: *(goes over to Gina, who stands by the stove, and says in a low voice)* No more lies, please. If everything was over between you and him when you—when you began to love me, as you call it—why did he make it possible for us to marry?

GINA: I suppose he thought he could come and go at his pleasure.

HJALMAR: Only that? Wasn't he afraid of a certain possibility?

GINA: I don't know what you mean.

HJALMAR: I want to know whether—your child has the right to live under my roof.

GINA: *(draws herself up; her eyes flash)* How can you ask that!

HJALMAR: You will answer this question: Does Hedvig belong to me—or to—? Answer!

GINA: *(looking at him with cold defiance)* I don't know.

HJALMAR: *(quivering a little)* You don't know!

GINA: How should I know? A woman like me—

116

HJALMAR: *(quietly turning away from her)* Then there is nothing left for me in this house.

GREGERS: Be careful, Hjalmar! Think what you're doing!

HJALMAR: *(puts on his overcoat)* There is nothing left for a man like me to think about in this situation.

GREGERS: But there are many things to think about. You must all stay together if you are going reach the goal of selfless forgiveness.

HJALMAR: I have no desire to reach that goal. Never, never! My hat! *(takes his hat)* My house has fallen in ruins about me. *(bursts into tears)* Gregers, I have no child!

HEDVIG: *(who has opened the kitchen door)* What are you saying? *(coming to him)* Daddy, daddy!

GINA: You see what's happening!

HJALMAR: Don't come near me, Hedvig! Go away. I can't bear to look at you. Oh! those eyes—! *(makes for the door)*

HEDVIG: *(clinging to him and screaming loudly)* No! no! Don't leave me!

GINA: *(cries out)* Look at the child, Ekdal! Look at the child!

HJALMAR: I won't! I can't! I have to get out—away from all this! *(he tears himself away from Hedvig and goes out by the passage door)*

HEDVIG: *(with despairing eyes)* He's leaving us, mother! He's leaving us! He'll never come back again!

GINA: Don't cry, Hedvig. Daddy will be back.

HEDVIG: *(throws herself sobbing on the sofa)* No, no, he'll never come home again.

GREGERS: Please believe I meant well, Mrs. Ekdal.

GINA: Maybe you did. But God forgive you.

HEDVIG: *(lying on the floor)* I think this will kill me! What did I do to him? Mother, you must get him home again!

GINA: Yes, yes, yes. Only be quiet, and I'll go out and look for him. *(puts on her outdoor things)* Maybe he's gone to Relling. But promise you won't lie there and cry. Promise me!

HEDVIG: *(weeping convulsively)* Yes, I'll stop, I won't cry—if only daddy comes back!

GREGERS: *(to Gina, who is going)* Wouldn't it be better to let him fight his bitter fight to the end?

GINA: He can do that later. First, we have to quiet the child. *(goes out by the passage door)*

HEDVIG: *(sits up and dries her tears)* Now you have to tell me what all this means. Why doesn't daddy want me any more?

GREGERS: Don't ask that until you're a big girl— quite grown-up.

HEDVIG: *(sobs)* I can't go on being this miserable until I'm a grown-up. —I think I know what it is. Maybe I'm not really daddy's child.

GREGERS: *(uneasily)* How could that be?

HEDVIG: Maybe mother found me. And maybe daddy just found out about it. I've read about such things.

GREGERS: Well, even so—

HEDVIG: I think he might love me in spite of that. He might even love me more. The wild duck was a present, you know, but I love it all the same.

GREGERS: *(turning the conversation)* Ah, the wild duck, that's true! Let's talk a bit about the wild duck, Hedvig.

HEDVIG: My poor wild duck! He doesn't want to look at it any more either. You know, he wanted to wring her neck!

GREGERS: Oh, he'd never do that.

HEDVIG: No, but he said it. And I think it was disgusting of my father to say it. I pray for the wild duck every night. I pray for her to be preserved from death and anything evil.

GREGERS: *(looking at her)* Do you say your prayers every night?

HEDVIG: Of course.

GREGERS: Who taught you to do that?

HEDVIG: I taught myself. Once when daddy was very sick, and they put leeches on his neck, and he said death was staring him in the face. . . .

GREGERS: Yes?

HEDVIG: I prayed for him then in my bed. And I've prayed ever since.

GREGERS: And now you pray for the wild duck too?

HEDVIG: I thought it would be best to pray for the wild duck, because she was so weak at first.

GREGERS: Do you pray in the morning too?

HEDVIG: No, of course not.

GREGERS: Why not pray in the morning too?

HEDVIG: It's light in the morning, you know, and so there's nothing to be afraid of then.

GREGERS: And your father wanted to wring the neck of the wild duck that you love so dearly?

HEDVIG: No, he said that he ought to wring her neck, but that he would spare her for my sake. That was kind of daddy.

GREGERS: *(coming a little nearer)* But suppose you sacrificed the wild duck for him of your own free will.

HEDVIG: *(rising)* The wild duck!

GREGERS: Suppose you were to give him a free-will offering of the dearest treasure you have in the world!

HEDVIG: Do you think that would help?

GREGERS: Try it, Hedvig.

HEDVIG: *(softly, with flashing eyes)* Yes, I will try it.

GREGERS: Do you think you really have the courage for it?

HEDVIG: I will ask grandfather to shoot the wild duck for me.

GREGERS: Yes, you do that. But don't say a word to your mother.

HEDVIG: Why not?

GREGERS: She doesn't understand us.

HEDVIG: The wild duck! I'll do it tomorrow morning.

(Gina comes in by the passage door.)

HEDVIG: *(going toward her)* Did you find him, mother?

GINA: No, but I was told he went out and took Relling with him.

GREGERS: Are you sure?

GINA: Yes, the concierge said so. She said Molvik went with them too.

GREGERS: Tonight, when he needs solitude so much to wrestle with his thoughts—!

GINA: *(takes off her things)* Yes, you can never tell about men. God only knows where Relling has dragged him to! I ran over to Madam Eriksen's, but they weren't there.

HEDVIG: *(struggling to keep back her tears)* What if he never comes again!

GREGERS: He'll come home again. I will have news to give him tomorrow, and then you'll see how he comes home. Depend on it, Hedvig, and sleep in peace. Good night. *(he goes out by the passage door)*

HEDVIG: *(throws herself sobbing on Gina's neck)* Mother, mother!

GINA: *(pats her shoulder and sighs)* Yes, yes; Relling was right. This is what happens when crazy creatures go around with their claims of—their claims of—whatever you call it.

ACT 5

Hjalmar Ekdal's studio. Cold, grey morning light. Wet snow lies on the skylight of the atelier.

Gina comes from the kitchen with an apron, carrying a broom and a duster. She goes toward the sitting room door. At the same moment Hedvig comes hurrying in from the passage.

GINA: *(stops)* Well?

HEDVIG: Oh, mother, I think he's downstairs with Relling—

GINA: Isn't that something!

HEDVIG: —because the porter's wife says she heard two people come in with Relling late last night.

GINA: Just what I thought.

HEDVIG: But what use is that, if he won't come home?

GINA: I'll go and have a talk with him.

(Old Ekdal, in dressing gown and slippers, and with a lighted pipe, appears at the door of his room.)

EKDAL: Look, Hjalmar— Isn't Hjalmar home?

GINA: No, he's gone out.

EKDAL: So early? And in such a heavy snowstorm? Well, well, that's his business. I'll take my morning walk alone. *(He slides the storeroom door aside; Hedvig helps him. He goes in; she closes it after him.)*

122

HEDVIG: *(in an undertone)* Just think what poor grandfather will say when he hears that father wants to leave us.

GINA: Nonsense. Grandfather mustn't hear anything about it. I thank God he wasn't home yesterday in the midst of all that fuss.

HEDVIG: Yes, but—

(Gregers comes in by the passage door.)

GREGERS: Well. Any news yet?

GINA: They say he's down with Relling.

GREGERS: With Relling! Was he really out with those people?

GINA: Apparently he was.

GREGERS: When what he needs most is solitude, to collect and clear his thoughts—

GINA: Yes, you can say that all right.

(Relling enters from the passage.)

HEDVIG: *(going to him)* Is daddy in your room?

GINA: *(at the same time)* Is he there?

RELLING: Yes, he certainly is.

HEDVIG: And you didn't tell us!

RELLING: Yes, I'm a brute. But I had to look after that other brute. I mean our demonic friend. And then I passed out and—

GINA: What does Ekdal have to say today?

RELLING: Nothing whatsoever.

HEDVIG: He doesn't say anything?

RELLING: Not a single word.

GREGERS: Of course he doesn't. That makes sense to me.

GINA: But what's he doing then?

RELLING: Lying on the sofa, snoring.

GINA: Oh yes, Ekdal is good at snoring.

HEDVIG: He's asleep? Is he able to sleep?

RELLING: It sure looks like it.

GREGERS: That's easy to understand, when such a profound spiritual conflict has torn him to—

GINA: Besides, he's not used to staying up so late.

HEDVIG: Maybe it's good he's getting some sleep, mother.

GINA: Sure it is. And we don't want to wake him up too soon. Thank you, Relling. I have to clean and tidy up the house a bit first, and then— Come help me, Hedvig. *(Gina and Hedvig go into the living room)*

GREGERS: *(turning to Relling)* What do you say about the spiritual crisis that Hjalmar Ekdal is suffering?

RELLING: I haven't noticed any spiritual crisis in him.

GREGERS: What! After his whole life has been placed on a new foundation? How can you believe that such a strong personality as Hjalmar—?

RELLING: Him? A strong personality? If he ever developed anything so abnormal as what you call a personality, I can assure you it was rooted out of him when he was still in his teens.

GREGERS: I would find that very strange—considering how he was brought up with such loving care.

124

RELLING: What? You mean those two batty, hysterical maiden aunts?

GREGERS: Let me inform you that these were women who never ignored the claim of the ideal—but of course that will only raise your scorn again.

RELLING: No, I'm in no mood for scorn. I know all about those ladies. He's discharged no end of bombast about those "two soul-mothers." But in my opinion he has very little to thank them for. Ekdal's misfortune is that he has always been considered a shining light in his own circle—

GREGERS: For very good reason. Consider the depth of his intellect!

RELLING: That's escaped me. His father believed in it, of course, but then the old lieutenant has always been an ass.

GREGERS: All his life he has had a childlike mind. But that's something you'll never understand.

RELLING: That may be. But when our dear, sweet Hjalmar went to college, he was also treated as the shining light of the future by his fellow students. The idiot was handsome—pink and white —a shop girl's dream of male beauty. And with that facile emotionalism, and that sympathetic voice, and that talent for declaiming other people's verses and other people's thoughts—

GREGERS: (indignantly) Is it really Hjalmar Ekdal you are talking about this way?

RELLING: Yes, if you please. I'm simply giving you a good look at the idol you've been groveling before.

GREGERS: I hardly think I've been as blind as that.

RELLING: The hell you say—you're not far from it. You're a sick man too, you know.

GREGERS: You're right there.

RELLING: Yes. But yours is a complicated case. First of all, you have this acute case of integrity and then, what's worse, you're always delirious with hero worship. You're in constant need of something to adore, outside yourself.

GREGERS: Yes, I have to look for it outside myself.

RELLING: But you're always so miserably wrong about every new miracle worker you think you've discovered. One more time you've entered a worker's home with your claim of the ideal, but the people in this house are all bankrupt.

GREGERS: If that's your opinion of Hjalmar Ekdal, why are you always hanging around with him?

RELLING: Well, you see, I'm supposed to be a kind of a doctor, God help me! I have no choice but to help the poor sickies who live in the same house with me.

GREGERS: Oh really! So Hjalmar Ekdal is sick too!

RELLING: Most people are, unfortunately.

GREGERS: And what's your prescription in Hjalmar's case?

RELLING: My usual one. I am cultivating his life lie.

GREGERS: His life lie? I don't think I heard what you said.

RELLING: I said life lie. The life lie, you know, is the animating principle of life.

GREGERS: May I ask what kind of life lie Hjalmar Ekdal suffers from?

126

RELLING: Sorry. I don't betray professional secrets to quacks. You'd probably go and screw him up even more than you have already. But my method is infallible. I have applied it to Molvik too. I have made him "demonic." That's the plaster I put on *his* boil.

GREGERS: He's not demonic then?

RELLING: What the hell does it mean, demonic! It's only a piece of gibberish I invented to keep him alive. If he didn't have that, the poor wretch would have given way to self-contempt and despair a long time ago. And then there's the old lieutenant! But he discovered his cure by himself, you see.

GREGERS: Lieutenant Ekdal? What about him?

RELLING: Just think of that old bear hunter shutting himself up in a dark storeroom and shooting rabbits! There isn't a happier sportsman in the whole world than that pathetic old man pottering around in that scrap heap. Those four or five withered Christmas trees he keeps are the same to him as the whole fresh Hoidal forest. The cocks and the hens are his wild birds in the treetops. And the rabbits that flop about the storeroom floor represent the big game he has to challenge—the mighty mountain hunter!

GREGERS: Unlucky old Lieutenant Ekdal, yes! It's true he has had to limit his youthful ideals.

RELLING: While we're at it, Mr. Werle, junior—get rid of that foreign word, *ideals*. We have a better native term: *lies*.

GREGERS: You think those two words are the same?

RELLING: Almost the same as typhus and putrid fever.

GREGERS: Dr. Relling, I will not give up until I have rescued Hjalmar from your influence!

RELLING: So much the worse for him. Rob the average man of his life lie, and you rob him of his happiness. *(to Hedvig, who comes in from the sitting room)* So, little wild-duck mother. I'm going down to see if your papa is still lying on his back, meditating on his wonderful invention. *(goes out by passage door)*

GREGERS: *(approaches Hedvig)* I can tell by your face that you haven't done it yet.

HEDVIG: What? Oh, you mean about the wild duck! No.

GREGERS: Your courage failed you when the time came, no?

HEDVIG: No, that's not it. It's just that when I woke up this morning and thought about what you said, it seemed so peculiar.

GREGERS: Peculiar?

HEDVIG: Yes, I don't know. Last night, at the time, it seemed like such a wonderful idea. But after I slept and thought about it again, it didn't seem the same.

GREGERS: Oh no, you just can't grow up in this house without being maimed.

HEDVIG: I don't care about that, if only daddy would come back—

GREGERS: Oh, if only your eyes were opened to what gives life its true value. If only you had the joyous, fearless spirit of sacrifice, you would know how to bring him back to you. But I still think you can, Hedvig.

(He goes out by the outside door. Hedvig wanders about the room for a time. She is about to go into the kitchen when a knock is heard at the attic door. Hedvig goes over and opens it a little; old Ekdal comes out; she pushes the door shut again.)

EKDAL: Hm, it's no fun taking a morning walk alone.

HEDVIG: Do you want to do some shooting, grandfather?

EKDAL: It's the wrong weather for shooting today. It's too dark in there; you can hardly see where you're going.

HEDVIG: Do you ever want to shoot anything besides rabbits?

EKDAL: Aren't rabbits good enough?

HEDVIG: Yes, but what about the wild duck?

EKDAL: Ho! Ho! You're afraid I'll shoot your wild duck? Never in a million years. Never.

HEDVIG: No, I guess you couldn't. Wild ducks are too difficult to shoot.

EKDAL: Couldn't! I sure could.

HEDVIG: How would you do it, grandfather? I don't mean my wild duck, but the others?

EKDAL: You shoot them in the breast, you know. That's the surest place. And then you have to shoot against the feathers, you see—not in the lie of the feathers.

HEDVIG: Does that make them die, grandfather?

EKDAL: Of course that makes them die—when you shoot properly. Well, I have to go and clean up a little. Hm—you understand—hm. *(goes into his room)*

129

(Hedvig waits a little, glances toward the sitting room door, goes over to the bookcase, stands on tiptoe, takes the double-barreled pistol down from the shelf, and looks at it. Gina, with brush and duster, comes from the sitting room. Hedvig hastily lays down the pistol, unobserved.)

GINA: Don't get into your father's things, Hedvig.

HEDVIG: *(goes away from the bookcase)* I was only cleaning up a little.

GINA: You'd better go into the kitchen and see if the coffee's still hot. I'll take him a breakfast tray when I go down.

(Hedvig goes out. Gina begins to sweep and clean up the studio. Presently the passage door is opened with hesitation, and Hjalmar Ekdal looks in. His overcoat is on, but not his hat; he is unwashed, and his hair is disheveled and unkempt. His eyes are dull and heavy.)

GINA: *(standing with the brush in her hand and looking at him)* Oh, there you are, Ekdal. So you've come home?

HJALMAR: *(comes in and answers in a toneless voice)* I have come home—but I'm going away immediately.

GINA: Yes, yes, I suppose so. But, Lord, Lord, what a sight you are!

HJALMAR: A sight?

GINA: And your best overcoat too! What a mess.

HEDVIG: *(at the kitchen door)* Mother, do you think I should—? *(sees Hjalmar, gives a loud scream of joy, and runs to him)* Oh, daddy, daddy!

HJALMAR: *(turns away with a gesture of revulsion)* Go

130

away! Go away! *(to Gina)* Keep her away from me, I tell you!

GINA: *(in a low tone)* Go into the living room, Hedvig. *(Hedvig does so without a word)*

HJALMAR: *(fussily pulls out the table drawer, trying to look busy)* I want my books with me. Where are my books?

GINA: Which books?

HJALMAR: My scientific books, of course, the technical journals I need for my invention.

GINA: *(searches in the bookcase)* These, the unbound ones?

HJALMAR: Of course.

GINA: *(lays a heap of magazines on the table)* Do you want Hedvig to cut the pages for you?

HJALMAR: I don't need to have them cut for me. *(short silence)*

GINA: Then you're still going to leave us, Ekdal?

HJALMAR: *(rummaging among the books)* That goes without saying.

GINA: Well, well.

HJALMAR: *(vehemently)* How can I still live here with a knife in my heart every hour of the day?

GINA: God forgive you for believing such bad things about me.

HJALMAR: Give me some proof—!

GINA: I think it's you that's got to prove.

HJALMAR: After a past like yours? There are certain claims—I could almost call them claims of the ideal—

131

GINA: What about grandfather? What's going to become of him, poor dear?

HJALMAR: I know my duty. The poor helpless man will come with me. I am going into town to make arrangements. Hm— *(hesitatingly)* has any one found my hat on the stairs?

GINA: No. Did you lose your hat?

HJALMAR: Of course I'm sure I had it on when I came in last night, no doubt about it. But this morning I couldn't find it.

GINA: Good God! Where did you go with those two drunks?

HJALMAR: Don't bother me about trifles. Do you suppose I am in any condition to remember details?

GINA: I hope you haven't caught cold, Ekdal— *(goes out into the kitchen)*

HJALMAR: *(talks to himself in a low tone of irritation while he empties the table drawer)* You're a bastard, Relling! A low human being! Oh, you shameless seducer! —I'd like to get someone to stick a knife in you! *(He lays some old letters on one side. He finds the torn document of yesterday, takes it up and looks at the pieces, and puts it down hurriedly as Gina enters.)*

GINA: *(sets a tray with coffee, etc. on the table)* Here's something hot, if you'd want. And there's some bread and butter and a bit of sausage.

HJALMAR: *(glancing at the tray)* Sausage? Never under this roof! It's true I haven't had a mouthful of solid food for almost twenty-four hours, but never mind. —My notes! The first pages of my memoirs! What's become of my diary and all my important papers? *(opens the sitting room door but draws back)* There she is again!

132

GINA: My God! The child has to be somewhere!

HJALMAR: Come out. *(He makes room. Hedvig comes, scared, into the studio.)*

HJALMAR: *(with his hand on the door handle, says to Gina)* During the last moments I am spending in my former home, I would like to be spared the presence of outsiders— *(goes into the room)*

HEDVIG: *(with a bound toward her mother, asks softly, trembling)* Does he mean me?

GINA: Stay in the kitchen, Hedvig. *(speaks to Hjalmar as she goes in to him)* Wait a second, Ekdal. Don't turn it all upside down. I know where everything is.

HEDVIG: *(stands a moment immovable, in terror and perplexity, biting her lips to keep back the tears; then she clenches her hands convulsively and says softly)* The wild duck. *(She steals over and takes the pistol from the shelf, opens the attic door a little way, creeps in, and shuts the door after her. Hjalmar and Gina can be heard arguing in the sitting room.)*

HJALMAR: *(comes in with some manuscript books and old loose papers, which he lays on the table)* This briefcase is useless! I have a thousand and one things to take with me.

GINA: *(following with the folder)* Why not let the rest wait? Just take a shirt and a pair of underwear with you?

HJALMAR: Whew! All these exhausting preparations—! *(pulls off his overcoat and throws it on the sofa)*

GINA: And there's your coffee getting cold.

HJALMAR: Hm. *(drinks a mouthful without thinking of it, and then another)*

GINA: *(dusting the back of the chairs)* It won't be easy finding another big storage room for the rabbits.

HJALMAR: What! Am I to supposed to drag all those rabbits with me too?

GINA: You don't think grandfather can get along without his rabbits.

HJALMAR: He'll have to get used to it. Haven't I sacrificed a lot more than rabbits?!

GINA: *(dusting the bookcase)* Shall I put the recorder in the briefcase for you?

HJALMAR: No. No recorder. But give me the pistol!

GINA: You want to take a gun with you?

HJALMAR: Yes. My loaded pistol.

GINA: *(searching for it)* It's not here. He must have taken it in with him.

HJALMAR: Is he in the storeroom?

GINA: Of course he's in the storeroom.

HJALMAR: Hm—poor lonely man. *(he takes a piece of bread and butter, eats it, and finishes his cup of coffee)*

GINA: If we hadn't rented the other room, you could have moved in there.

HJALMAR: And stayed under the same roof with—! Never, never!

GINA: But couldn't you try the living room for a day or two? You could have it all to yourself.

HJALMAR: Never within these walls!

GINA: Well, what about downstairs, with Relling and Molvik.

HJALMAR: Don't mention their loathsome names to

me! The very thought of them makes me almost lose my appetite. No, I have to go out into the storm and snow, I must go from house to house, seeking shelter for my father and me.

GINA: But you don't have a hat, Ekdal! You've lost your hat, you know.

HJALMAR: Oh those scum, those slaves of all the vices! I must find a hat. *(takes another piece of bread and butter)* I must make the necessary arrangements. I can't throw away my life, you know. *(looks for something on the tray)*

GINA: What are you looking for?

HJALMAR: Butter.

GINA: I'll get some for you. *(goes out into the kitchen)*

HJALMAR: *(calls after her)* Oh, don't bother, dry bread is good enough for me.

GINA: *(brings a dish of butter)* Look, this is nice and fresh. *(She pours another cup of coffee for him. He seats himself on the couch, spreads more butter on the already buttered bread, and eats and drinks awhile in silence.)*

HJALMAR: Do you think I could—without being intruded on by anyone—do you think I could stay in the living room for a day or two?

GINA: Sure you could, if you wanted to.

HJALMAR: Because it's impossible for me to get all of father's things out of here in such a short time.

GINA: And besides, you haven't told him yet you don't want to live with us any more.

HJALMAR: *(pushes away his coffee cup)* Yes, that's another thing. I'll have to reveal the whole messy story. I must have time to think things over. I must have time to breathe. I can't assume all these burdens in a single day.

GINA: No, especially when it's so miserable outside.

HJALMAR: *(touching Werle's letter)* I see that letter is still lying here.

GINA: Yes, I haven't touched it.

HJALMAR: So far as I am concerned it's just trash—

GINA: Well, I'm certainly not going to do anything with it.

HJALMAR: But we'd better not lose it anyway. In the mess of moving, it might easily—

GINA: I'll take care of it, Ekdal.

HJALMAR: The gift has been made first to my father, and it's up to him to accept it or reject it.

GINA: *(sighs)* Yes, poor grandfather—

HJALMAR: Just to be safe. Where can I find some glue?

GINA: *(goes to the bookcase)* Here's the gluepot.

HJALMAR: And a brush?

GINA: Here's a brush too. *(brings him the things)*

HJALMAR: *(takes a pair of scissors)* Just a strip of paper at the back. *(clips and glues)* Far be it from me to meddle with other people's property, especially what belongs to a destitute old man. And to—to that other person too. There. Let it stay for a while, and when it dries, take it away. I don't want to see that document ever again. Never!

(Gregers Werle enters from the passage.)

GREGERS: *(somewhat surprised)* What are you doing here, Hjalmar?

HJALMAR: *(rises hurriedly)* I had collapsed from fatigue.

GREGERS: You've been having breakfast, I see.

HJALMAR: The body sometimes has its claims as well.

GREGERS: What have you decided to do?

HJALMAR: For a man like me, there's only one possible course. I'm just collecting my most important things. It takes time, you know.

GINA: *(with a touch of impatience)* Do you want me to get the room ready for you, or pack your suitcase?

HJALMAR: *(after a glance of annoyance at Gregers)* Pack—and get it ready!

GINA: *(takes the suitcase)* All right, I'll put in your other things. *(goes into the living room and closes the door after her)*

GREGERS: *(after a short silence)* I never thought it would come to this. Do you really think it's necessary to leave your home?

HJALMAR: *(wanders about restlessly)* What else would you have me do? I'm not built for unhappiness, Gregers. I must feel secure and peaceful in my surroundings.

GREGERS: But can't you have that here? Just try. I would think you have firm ground to build on now—with a fresh start. And remember, you have your invention to live for.

HJALMAR: Oh, don't talk about my invention. It's still a long way off.

GREGERS: Really!

137

HJALMAR: My God, what do you want me to invent? Almost everything has been invented already. Every day it becomes harder and harder—

GREGERS: But you've worked so hard at it.

HJALMAR: It was that bastard Relling who started me on it.

GREGERS: Relling?

HJALMAR: Yes, he was the one who first made me realize I had a talent for making some important invention in photography.

GREGERS: So it was Relling!

HJALMAR: And it made me so happy, Gregers! Not the invention so much as the fact that Hedvig believed in it—with a child's trusting, wholehearted faith. At least, I was stupid enough to imagine that she believed in it.

GREGERS: Do you really think that Hedvig wasn't honest about it?

HJALMAR: I can think anything now. It is Hedvig who stands in my way. She has blocked all the sunlight from my life.

GREGERS: Hedvig! Are you talking about Hedvig? How could she block out your sunlight?

HJALMAR: (without answering) How deeply I have loved that child! How profoundly happy I felt every time I came home to my poor room and she ran in to meet me, with her sweet little shuttered eyes. Stupid fool that I am! I loved her passionately—and I gave myself up to the dream, the delusion, that she loved me passionately in return.

GREGERS: You call that a delusion?

HJALMAR: How should I know? I can't get anything out of Gina, and besides, she's totally blind to the ideal side of all these complications. But I have to tell you what's on my mind, Gregers. I can't shake off this terrible doubt. Maybe Hedvig has never really loved me.

GREGERS: Perhaps she could prove it to you in some way. *(listens)* What's that? I thought I heard the wild duck—?

HJALMAR: The wild duck is quacking. My father's in the storeroom.

GREGERS: He is? *(his face lights up with joy)* You may yet have proof that your poor misunderstood Hedvig truly loves you!

HJALMAR: Oh, what proof could she possibly give me? I can't expect any reassurance from that quarter.

GREGERS: Hedvig does not know the word deceit.

HJALMAR: Oh, Gregers, that's just what I can never know. Who can say what Gina and Mrs. Soerby may have been whispering and gossiping about here? And Hedvig always has her ears open, I can tell you. Perhaps that deed of gift wasn't such a surprise to her, after all. In fact, I think I noticed something like that.

GREGERS: What in the world has gotten into you?

HJALMAR: My eyes have been opened. Just wait. You'll see that deed of gift is just the beginning. Mrs. Soerby has always liked Hedvig a lot, and now she's in a position to do anything she likes for the child. They can take her away from me whenever they please.

GREGERS: Hedvig will never, never leave you.

HJALMAR: Don't be so sure. All they have to do is beckon and throw out some golden bait—! And I have loved her so much! I would have wanted nothing more than to take her tenderly by the hand and lead her through life, as one takes a frightened child through a big dark empty room! Now I am certain that the poor photographer in his humble attic has never really meant anything to her. She has only been cunning enough to humor him until the time came.

GREGERS: You don't really believe that, Hjalmar.

HJALMAR: That's what is so terrible. I don't know what I believe. And I never will know. But do you really doubt what I'm saying? Ha ha, you've banked too much on the claim of the ideal, my good Gregers! If those others came, with all their wealth and glamour, and said to the child, "Leave him and come to us. This is where your life is!"—

GREGERS: *(quickly)* Well, what do you think would happen?

HJALMAR: If then I asked her: Hedvig, would you be willing to renounce that life for me? *(laughs scornfully)* No, thank you! You'd soon hear what answer I'd get.

(A pistol shot is heard from within the garret.)

GREGERS: *(loudly and joyfully)* Hjalmar!

HJALMAR: Listen to that. He has to go hunting now.

GINA: *(comes in)* Hjalmar, I think grandfather is messing around in the storeroom by himself.

HJALMAR: I'll take a look—

GREGERS: *(eagerly, with emotion)* Wait! Do you know what that was?

HJALMAR: Of course I do.

GREGERS: No, you don't. But I do. That was the proof!

HJALMAR: What proof?

GREGERS: The free offering of a child. She got your father to shoot the wild duck.

HJALMAR: To shoot the wild duck!

GINA: Oh, what a thought—!

HJALMAR: But what for?

GREGERS: She wanted to sacrifice—for you—the thing she loved most, because she thought it would make you love her again.

HJALMAR: *(tenderly, with emotion)* Oh, poor child!

GINA: What things get into her head!

GREGERS: She only wanted your love again, Hjalmar. She couldn't live without it.

GINA: *(struggling with her tears)* There, you see, Ekdal?

HJALMAR: Where is she, Gina?

GINA: *(sniffs)* Poor dear, she's probably sitting in the kitchen.

HJALMAR: *(goes over, tears open the kitchen door, and says)* Hedvig, come to me! *(looks around)* No, she's not here.

HJALMAR: *(outside)* No, she's not there either. *(comes in)* She must have gone out.

GINA: Yes, you didn't want her in the house.

HJALMAR: Oh, if only she'd come home so, so I could tell her—. Everything will be all right now, Gregers. Now I believe we can start life over again.

GREGERS: *(quietly)* I knew it. I knew the child would make things right.

(Old Ekdal appears at the door of his room. He is in full uniform and is busy buckling on his sword.)

HJALMAR: *(astonished)* Father! What are you doing here?

GINA: Have you been shooting in your room?

EKDAL: *(resentfully, approaching)* So you've been shooting without me, Hjalmar?

HJALMAR: *(excited and confused)* It wasn't you who fired that shot in the storeroom?

EKDAL: Me? Hm.

GREGERS: *(calls out to Hjalmar)* She's shot the wild duck herself!

HJALMAR: What can it mean? *(he hurries to the attic door, tears it open, looks in, and calls loudly)* Hedvig!

GINA: *(runs to the door)* Good God, what is it?!

HJALMAR: *(goes in)* She's lying on the floor!

GREGERS: Hedvig! On the floor! *(goes in to Hjalmar)*

GINA: *(at the same time)* Hedvig! Inside the storeroom, No, no, no!

EKDAL: Ho-ho! So she goes shooting now too, eh?

(Hjalmar, Gina, and Gregers carry Hedvig into the studio. In her dangling right hand she holds the pistol clasped tightly in her fingers.)

HJALMAR: *(distracted)* The pistol's gone off. She shot herself. Call for help! Help!

GINA: *(runs into the passage and calls down)* Relling!

Relling! Doctor Relling, come as quick as you can!

(Hjalmar and Gregers lay Hedvig on the sofa.)

EKDAL: *(quietly)* The woods avenge themselves.

HJALMAR: *(on his knees beside Hedvig)* She's coming to now. She's coming to— Yes, yes, yes.

GINA: *(reenters)* Where did she shoot herself? I don't see anything—

(Relling comes hurriedly, and immediately after him Molvik, the latter without his waistcoat and necktie, and with his coat open.)

RELLING: What's going on here?

GINA: They say Hedvig has shot herself.

HJALMAR: Come and help us!

RELLING: Shot herself! *(he pushes the table aside and begins to examine her)*

HJALMAR: *(kneeling and looking anxiously up at him)* It can't be serious? Say something, Relling! She's hardly bleeding at all. It can't be serious?

RELLING: How did this happen?

HJALMAR: I have no idea—

GINA: She wanted to shoot the wild duck.

RELLING: The wild duck?

HJALMAR: The pistol must have gone off.

RELLING: Hm. I see.

EKDAL: The woods avenge themselves. But all the same, I'm not afraid. *(goes into the attic and closes the door after him)*

HJALMAR: Well, Relling—why don't you say something?

RELLING: The shot has entered her breast.

HJALMAR: Yes, but she's coming to!

RELLING: Surely you can see that Hedvig's dead.

GINA: *(bursts into tears)* Oh my child, my child—

GREGERS: *(huskily)* In the depths of the sea—

HJALMAR: *(jumps up)* No, no, she *must* live! For God's sake, Relling—just for a moment—just till I tell her how inexpressibly I loved her all the time!

RELLING: The bullet's gone through her heart. Internal hemorrhage. Death must have been instantaneous.

HJALMAR: And I drove her away from me! And she crept like a terrified animal into the storeroom and died for love of me! *(sobbing)* I can never make it up to her! I can never tell her—! *(clenches his hands and cries, upward)* God above—! If you are above! Why have you done this thing to me?

GINA: Be quiet, be quiet, don't go on this horrible way. We had no right to keep her, I suppose.

MOLVIK: The child is not dead but sleepeth.

RELLING: Bullshit.

HJALMAR: *(becomes calm, goes over to the sofa, folds his arms, and looks at Hedvig)* There she lies, so stiff and still.

RELLING: *(tries to loosen the pistol)* She's holding it so tight, so tight.

GINA: No, no, Relling, don't break her fingers. Let the gun alone.

HJALMAR: She has to take it with her.

GINA: Yes, let her. But the child mustn't lie here on display. She'll go into her own room, she will. Help me, Ekdal.

(Hjalmar and Gina take Hedvig between them.)

HJALMAR: *(as they are carrying her)* Oh, Gina, Gina, can you ever get over this!

GINA: We must help each other. Now I know she belongs to both of us.

MOLVIK: *(stretches out his arms and mumbles)* Blessed be the Lord. Earth to earth, and dust to dust—

RELLING: *(whispers)* Shut up, you fool, you're drunk.

(Hjalmar and Gina carry the body out through the kitchen door. Relling shuts it after them. Molvik slinks out into the passage.)

RELLING: *(goes over to Gregers and says)* No one will ever persuade me that this was an accident.

GREGERS: *(who has stood terrified, with convulsive twitchings)* No one can say how this terrible thing happened.

RELLING: The powder has burnt her dress. She must have pressed the pistol right against her breast and fired.

GREGERS: Hedvig has not died in vain. You saw how his grief has liberated all the best in him?

RELLING: Most people are ennobled by the presence of death. But how long do you think this nobility will last?

GREGERS: Surely it will endure and grow throughout his life?

RELLING: Within a year, little Hedvig will be nothing to him but a pretty theme for declamation.

GREGERS: How dare you say that about Hjalmar Ekdal?

RELLING: We'll discuss this again, when the first grass has grown over her grave. Then you'll hear him pontificating about "the child torn too early from her father's breast." Then you'll see him wallowing in the syrup of sentiment and self-admiration and self-pity. Just you wait!

GREGERS: If you're right and I am wrong, then life's not worth living.

RELLING: Oh, life would be quite bearable, after all, if only we were rid of those damned fools who keep badgering poor people with their "claim of the ideal."

GREGERS: *(looking straight before him)* If that's the case, then I'm glad I know what my destiny is.

RELLING: And what is your destiny, may I ask?

GREGERS: *(going)* To be the thirteenth at table.

RELLING: *(spits)* Oh, fuck you!